Crochet It. Love It. Wear It!

The Ultimate Collection for Every Occasion

LEISURE ARTS, INC.
Little Rock, Arkansas

Crochet It. Love It. Wear It!

EDITORIAL STAFF

Editor-in-Chief: Susan White Sullivan
Knit and Crochet Publications Director: Debra Nettles
Special Projects Director: Susan Frantz Wiles
Senior Prepress Director: Mark Hawkins
Art Publications Director: Rhonda Shelby
Technical Editor: Sarah J. Green
Contributing Editors: Linda Daley, Cathy Hardy, and Lois J. Long
Editorial Writer: Susan McManus Johnson
Art Category Manager: Lora Puls
Graphic Artists: Becca Snider, Amy Temple, Dana Vaughn, and Janie Marie Wright
Imaging Technicians: Stephanie Johnson and Mark R. Potter
Photography Manager: Katherine Laughlin
Contributing Photographer: Jason Masters
Contributing Photostylist: Cora Holdaway
Publishing Systems Administrator: Becky Riddle
Publishing Systems Assistant: Clint Hanson
Mac Information Technology Specialist: Robert Young

BUSINESS STAFF

Vice President and Chief Operations Officer: Tom Siebenmorgen
Director of Finance and Administration: Laticia Mull Dittrich
Vice President, Sales and Marketing: Pam Stebbins
Sales Director: Martha Adams
Marketing Director: Margaret Reinold
Creative Services Director: Jeff Curtis
Information Technology Director: Hermine Linz
Controller: Francis Caple
Vice President, Operations: Jim Dittrich
Comptroller, Operations: Rob Thieme
Retail Customer Service Manager: Stan Raynor
Print Production Manager: Fred F. Pruss

Library of Congress Control Number: 2010926120
ISBN-13: 978-1-60140-9-423
ISBN-10: 1-60140-9-427

TABLE OF CONTENTS

MEET THE CROCHET DUDE®

Drew Emborsky is one very busy dude! Fans of the hit PBS show "Knit and Crochet Today" know Drew as the program's crochet expert, while blog hoppers flock to Drew's wildly popular Web site at TheCrochetDude.com. The reason for all this interest is easy to see in this collection of clothing patterns: Drew has the gift of creating completely original fashions that are also practical. It's a talent he began developing at an early age.

"My mom taught me to crochet when I was five, when we were snowbound in Lake Tahoe," Drew says. "After studying fine art in college and doing the starving artist thing, I started crocheting for charity while grieving the passing of my mom. With the charity group, I became known as The Crochet Dude. This led to my blog, patterns in magazines and books, and appearances on TV."

Drew has appeared on a variety of HGTV and DIY television shows. He co-authored a book of knit fashions for men and their dogs and more recently published his own volume of crochet designs for men. TheCrochetDude.biz is an online stop where all "crochet dudes" are invited to join a conversation on the creative topic.

If you're interested in crocheting stylish and unique caps, dishcloths, bags, and pet accessories, Drew has four exciting new Leisure Arts Little Books: #75271 *In All Caps!*, #75272 *All Washed Up*, #75273 *Must Have Handbags*, and #75274 *Sweet Pet Comforts*. They're available from your local retailer and at LeisureArts.com.

For exciting new garments you'll adore, crochet these designs by Drew Emborsky—the world-famous Crochet Dude®! Drew created these patterns with plenty of figure-flattering shape and texture. Make a cardigan, vest, party dress, or pencil skirt that will accentuate your curves. Let a chic red coat take you out for a night on the town. There's even an ultra-feminine Little Black Dress that you simply must have. And don't forget the graceful openwork skirt to wear over your best skinny pants! Sweet details and sophisticated styling are yours to enjoy with each garment as you crochet, wear, and love it!

DEBRA

One of my earliest memories of crochet fashion was a wonderful long cardigan that my sister Debra crocheted. She worked it in blues and greens and I often wonder if that was when those colors became my faves! Here is an updated version using all-over cables and a solid color.

■■■□ INTERMEDIATE

Size	Finished Chest Measurement
Small	34¹/₂" (87.5 cm)
Medium	36³/₄" (93.5 cm)
Large	40³/₄" (10.5 cm)
X-Large	42³/₄" (108.5 cm)
2X-Large	44³/₄" (113.5 cm)

Size Note: Instructions are written with sizes Small and Medium in the first set of braces { } and sizes Large, X-Large, and 2X-Large in the second set of braces. Instructions will be easier to read if you circle all the numbers pertaining to your size. If only one number is given, it applies to all sizes.

MATERIALS
Medium Weight Yarn ④
[3.5 ounces, 215 yards
(100 grams, 197 meters) per skein]:
  {12-13}{15-17-19} skeins
Crochet hook, size G (4 mm) **or** size needed
  for gauge
Split-ring marker
Yarn needle

Photo model made using Brown Sheep Company, Inc. Cotton Fleece CW850 Berry.

GAUGES: In Lower Body pattern,
17 sts and 10 rows = 4" (10 cm)
In Upper Body pattern,
12 sts and 8 rows = 4" (10 cm)

Gauge Swatch: 4"w x 4¹/₄"h (10 cm x 10.75 cm)
Ch 18.
Rows 1-11: Work same as Lower Body, page 8: 17 sts. Finish off.

STITCH GUIDE
TREBLE CROCHET *(abbreviated tr)*
YO twice, insert hook in st indicated, YO and pull up a loop (4 loops on hook), (YO and draw through 2 loops on hook) 3 times.
BACK POST DOUBLE CROCHET *(abbreviated BPdc)*
YO, insert hook from **back** to **front** around post of st indicated *(Fig. 4, page 95)*, YO and pull up a loop (3 loops on hook), (YO and draw through 2 loops on hook) twice.
FRONT POST DOUBLE CROCHET *(abbreviated FPdc)*
YO, insert hook from **front** to **back** around post of st indicated *(Fig. 4, page 95)*, YO and pull up a loop (3 loops on hook), (YO and draw through 2 loops on hook) twice.
CABLE (uses next 2 sts)
Skip next st, work FPdc around next st, working in **front** of st just made, work FPdc around skipped st.
V-STITCH *(abbreviated V-St)*
(Dc, ch 1, dc) in st or sp indicated.

Instructions continued on page 8.

DEBRA

Body is worked in one piece to Armholes.

BODY
LOWER BODY
Ch {173-183}{203-213-223}.

Row 1: Sc in back ridge of second ch from hook and each ch across *(Fig. 1, page 95)*: {172-182} {202-212-222} sc.

Row 2 (Right side): Ch 2 **(counts as first hdc, now and throughout)**, turn; work FPdc around next sc, skip next sc, work V-St in next sc, ★ skip next 2 sc, dc in next sc, working **around** dc just made, dc in second skipped sc, skip next sc, work V-St in next sc; repeat from ★ across to last 3 sc, skip next sc, work FPdc around next sc, hdc in last sc: {34-36}{40-42-44} V-Sts.

Note: Loop a short piece of yarn around any stitch to mark Row 2 as **right** side.

Row 3: Ch 2, turn; work BPdc around next FPdc, work V-St in next V-St (ch-1 sp), (work BPdc around each of next 2 dc, work V-St in next V-St) across to last 2 sts, work BPdc around next FPdc, hdc in last hdc.

Row 4: Ch 2, turn; work FPdc around next BPdc, work V-St in next V-St, (work Cable, work V-St in next V-St) across to last 2 sts, work FPdc around next BPdc, hdc in last hdc.

Row 5: Ch 2, turn; work BPdc around next FPdc, work V-St in next V-St, (work BPdc around each of next 2 FPdc, work V-St in next V-St) across to last 2 sts, work BPdc around next FPdc, hdc in last hdc.

Repeat Rows 4 and 5 for pattern until Body measures approximately 18" (45.5 cm) from beginning ch, ending by working Row 4.

WAIST SHAPING
Row 1: Ch 2, turn; work BPdc around next FPdc, work V-St in next V-St, work BPdc around each of next 2 FPdc, work V-St in next V-St, ★ work BPdc around each of next 2 FPdc, dc in next V-St, work BPdc around each of next 2 FPdc, work V-St in next V-St; repeat from ★ across to last 2 sts, work BPdc around next FPdc, hdc in last hdc: {18-19}{21-22-23} V-Sts.

Row 2: Ch 2, turn; work FPdc around next BPdc, work V-St in next V-St, work Cable, ★ dc in next dc, work Cable, work V-St in next V-St, work Cable; repeat from ★ across to last V-St, work V-St in last V-St, work FPdc around next BPdc, hdc in last hdc.

Row 3: Ch 2, turn; work BPdc around next FPdc, dc in next V-St, work BPdc around each of next 2 FPdc, dc in next V-St, ★ work BPdc around each of next 2 FPdc, dc in next dc, work BPdc around each of next 2 FPdc, dc in next V-St; repeat from ★ across to last 2 sts, work BPdc around next FPdc, hdc in last hdc: {104-110}{122-128-134} sts.

UPPER BODY
Row 1: Ch 2, turn; work FPdc around next BPdc, dc in next dc, (work Cable, dc in next dc) across to last 2 sts, work FPdc around next BPdc, hdc in last hdc.

Row 2: Ch 2, turn; work BPdc around next FPdc, dc in next dc, (work BPdc around each of next 2 FPdc, dc in next dc) across to last 2 sts, work BPdc around next FPdc, hdc in last hdc.

Rows 3-12: Repeat Rows 1 and 2, 5 times; do **not** finish off.

RIGHT FRONT
Row 1: Ch 2, turn; work FPdc around next BPdc, (dc in next dc, work Cable) {6-7}{8-8-9} times, hdc in next dc, leave remaining sts unworked: {21-24}{27-27-30} sts.

Row 2: Ch 2, turn; (work BPdc around each of next 2 FPdc, dc in next dc) across to last 2 sts, work BPdc around next FPdc, hdc in last hdc.

Row 3 (Decrease row): Ch 2, turn; work FPdc around next BPdc, skip next dc, work Cable, (dc in next dc, work Cable) across to last hdc, hdc in last hdc: {20-23}{26-26-29} sts.

Row 4: Ch 2, turn; (work BPdc around each of next 2 FPdc, dc in next dc) across to last 4 sts, work BPdc around each of next 3 FPdc, hdc in last hdc.

Row 5 (Decrease row): Ch 2, turn; work FPdc around next BPdc, skip next BPdc, work FPdc around next BPdc, (dc in next dc, work Cable) across to last hdc, hdc in last hdc: {19-22}{25-25-28} sts.

Row 6: Ch 2, turn; work BPdc around each of next 2 FPdc, (dc in next dc, work BPdc around each of next 2 FPdc) across to last hdc, hdc in last hdc.

Row 7 (Decrease row): Ch 2, turn; work FPdc around next BPdc, skip next BPdc, (dc in next dc, work Cable) across to last hdc, hdc in last hdc: {18-21}{24-24-27} sts.

Row 8: Ch 2, turn; (work BPdc around each of next 2 FPdc, dc in next dc) across to last 2 sts, work BPdc around next FPdc, hdc in last hdc.

Size Small Only
Rows 9-20: Repeat Rows 3-8 twice: 12 sts.

Finish off.

Sizes Medium, Large, X-Large and 2X-Large Only
Row 9: Repeat Row 3: {20}{23-23-26} sts.

Row 10 (Decrease row): Ch 2, turn; (work BPdc around each of next 2 FPdc, dc in next dc) across to last 4 sts, work BPdc around next FPdc, skip next FPdc, work BPdc around next FPdc, hdc in last hdc: {19}{22-22-25} sts.

Row 11: Repeat Row 7: {18}{21-21-24} sts.

Row 12 (Decrease row): Ch 2, turn; work BPdc around each of next 2 FPdc, (dc in next dc, work BPdc around next each of 2 FPdc) across to last 3 sts, skip next dc, work BPdc around next FPdc, hdc in last hdc: {17}{20-20-23} sts.

Row 13: Repeat Row 5: {16}{19-19-22} sts.

Row 14 (Decrease row): Ch 2, turn; (work BPdc around each of next 2 FPdc, dc in next dc) across to last 3 sts, skip next FPdc, work BPdc around next FPdc, hdc in last hdc: {15}{18-18-21} sts.

Size Medium Only
Rows 15-20: Repeat Rows 3-8: 12 sts.

Finish off.

Sizes Large, X-Large, and 2x-Large Only
Rows 15 thru {18-18-20}: Repeat Rows 9 thru {12-12-14}: {14-14-15} sts.

Rows {19-19-21} and {20-20-22}: Work even.

Finish off.

Instructions continued on page 10.

BACK

Sizes Small and Large Only

Row 1: With **right** side facing, skip next 10 sts from Right Front and join yarn with slip st in next BPdc; ch 2, dc in next dc, (work Cable, dc in next dc) {13}{15} times, hdc in next BPdc, leave remaining sts unworked: {42}{48} sts.

Row 2: Ch 2, turn; dc in next dc, (work BPdc around each of next 2 FPdc, dc in next dc) across to last hdc, hdc in last hdc.

Row 3: Ch 2, turn; dc in next dc, (work Cable, dc in next dc) across to last hdc, hdc in last hdc.

Sizes Medium, X-Large, and 2X-Large Only

Row 1: With **right** side facing, skip next 9 sts from Right Front and join yarn with slip st in next BPdc; ch 2, work FPdc around next BPdc, dc in next dc, (work Cable, dc in next dc) {13}{17-17} times, work FPdc around next BPdc, hdc in next BPdc, leave remaining sts unworked: {44}{56-56} sts.

Row 2: Ch 2, turn; work BPdc around next FPdc, dc in next dc, (work BPdc around each of next 2 FPdc, dc in next dc) across to last 2 sts, work BPdc around next FPdc, hdc in last hdc.

Row 3: Ch 2, turn; work FPdc around next BPdc, dc in next dc, (work Cable, dc in next dc) across to last 2 sts, work FPdc around next BPdc, hdc in last hdc.

All Sizes

Repeat Rows 2 and 3 for pattern until Back measures same as Right Front, ending by working a **wrong** side row; finish off.

LEFT FRONT

Row 1: With **right** side facing, skip next {10-9}{10-9-9} sts from Back and join yarn with slip st in next dc; ch 2, (work Cable, dc in next dc) across to last 2 sts, work FPdc around next BPdc, hdc in last hdc: {21-24}{27-27-30} sts.

Row 2: Ch 2, turn; work BPdc around next FPdc, (dc in next dc, work BPdc around each of next 2 FPdc) across to last hdc, hdc in last hdc.

Row 3 (Decrease row): Ch 2, turn; work Cable, (dc in next dc, work Cable) across to last 3 sts, skip next dc, work FPdc around next BPdc, hdc in last hdc: {20-23}{26-26-29} sts.

Row 4: Ch 2, turn; work BPdc around each of next 3 FPdc, (dc in next dc, work BPdc around each of next 2 FPdc) across to last hdc, hdc in last hdc.

Row 5 (Decrease row): Ch 2, turn; (work Cable, dc in next dc) across to last 4 sts, work FPdc around next BPdc, skip next BPdc, work FPdc around next BPdc, hdc in last hdc: {19-22}{25-25-28} sts.

Row 6: Ch 2, turn; work BPdc around each of next 2 FPdc, (dc in next dc, work BPdc around each of next 2 FPdc) across to last hdc, hdc in last hdc.

Row 7 (Decrease row): Ch 2, turn; (work Cable, dc in next dc) across to last 3 sts, skip next BPdc, work FPdc around next BPdc, hdc in last hdc: {18-21}{24-24-27} sts.

Row 8: Ch 2, turn; work BPdc around next FPdc, (dc in next dc, work BPdc around each of next 2 FPdc) across to last hdc, hdc in last hdc.

Size Small Only

Rows 9-20: Repeat Rows 3-8 twice: 12 sts.

Finish off.

Sizes Medium, Large, X-Large, and 2X-Large Only

Row 9: Repeat Row 3: {20}{23-23-26} sts.

Row 10 (Decrease row): Ch 2, turn; work BPdc around next FPdc, skip next FPdc, work BPdc around next FPdc, (dc in next dc, work BPdc around next 2 FPdc) across to last hdc, hdc in last hdc: {19}{22-22-25} sts.

Row 11: Repeat Row 7: {18}{21-21-24} sts.

Row 12 (Decrease row): Ch 2, turn; work BPdc around next FPdc, skip next dc, work BPdc around next 2 FPdc, (dc in next dc, work BPdc around next 2 FPdc) across to last hdc, hdc in last hdc: {17}{20-20-23} sts.

Row 13: Repeat Row 5: {16}{19-19-22} sts.

Row 14 (Decrease row): Ch 2, turn; work BPdc around next FPdc, skip next FPdc, (dc in next dc, work BPdc around each of next 2 FPdc) across to last hdc, hdc in last hdc: {15}{18-18-21} sts.

Size Medium Only
Rows 15-20: Repeat Rows 3-8: 12 sts.

Finish off.

Sizes Large, X-Large, and 2X-Large Only
Rows 15 thru {18-18-20}: Repeat Rows 9 thru {12-12-14}: {14-15-15} sts.

Rows {19-19-21} and {20-20-22}: Work even.

Finish off.

SLEEVE (Make 2)
CUFF
Ch {53-57}{61-69-73}, place marker in fourth ch from hook for st placement.

Row 1: Tr in back ridge of fifth ch from hook and each ch across: {50-54}{58-66-70} sts.

Row 2 (Right side): Ch 2, turn; (work FPdc around each of next 2 tr, work BPdc around each of next 2 tr) across to last tr, hdc in last tr.

Note: Mark Row 2 as **right** side.

Row 3: Ch 2, turn; work BPdc around next BPdc, work FPdc around each of next 2 sts, (work BPdc around each of next 2 sts, work FPdc around each of next 2 sts) across to last 2 sts, work BPdc around next FPdc, hdc in last hdc.

Row 4: Ch 2, turn; (work BPdc around each of next 2 sts, work FPdc around each of next 2 sts) across to last hdc, hdc in last hdc.

Row 5: Ch 2, turn; work FPdc around next FPdc, work BPdc around each of next 2 sts, (work FPdc around each of next 2 sts, work BPdc around each of next 2 sts) across to last 2 sts, work FPdc around next BPdc, hdc in last hdc.

Row 6: Ch 2, turn; (work FPdc around each of next 2 sts, work BPdc around each of next 2 sts) across to last hdc, hdc in last hdc.

Repeat Rows 3-6 for pattern until Cuff measures approximately 6" (15 cm) from beginning ch; finish off.

BODY
Row 1: With **right** side facing and working in free loops of beginning ch *(Fig. 3, page 95)*, join yarn with slip st in marked ch; ch 2, work FPdc around next tr, dc in next ch, (work Cable, dc in next ch) across to last {2-3}{4-3-4} sts, skip next {0-1}{2-1-2} ch(s) *(see Zeros, page 94)*, work FPdc around next tr, hdc in last ch: {50-53}{56-65-68} sts.

Row 2: Ch 2, turn; work BPdc around next FPdc, dc in next dc, (work BPdc around each of next 2 FPdc, dc in next dc) across to last 2 sts, work BPdc around next FPdc, hdc in last hdc.

Row 3: Ch 2, turn; work FPdc around next BPdc, dc in next dc, (work Cable, dc in next dc) across to last 2 sts, work FPdc around next BPdc, hdc in last hdc.

Repeat Rows 2 and 3 for pattern until Sleeve measures approximately {18-18³/₄}{19-19-19}"/ {45.5-47.5}{48.5-48.5-48.5} cm from beginning ch, ending by working Row 2.

Instructions continued on page 12.

SLEEVE CAP SHAPING
Maintain established pattern throughout.

Row 1 (Decrease row): Ch 2, turn; work FPdc around next BPdc, skip next dc, work Cable, (dc in next dc, work Cable) across to last 3 sts, skip next dc, work FPdc around next BPdc, hdc in last hdc: {48-51}{54-63-66} sts.

Row 2 (Decrease row): Ch 2, turn; skip next FPdc, work BPdc around each of next 2 FPdc, (dc in next dc, work BPdc around each of next 2 FPdc) across to last 2 sts, skip next FPdc, hdc in last hdc: {46-49}{52-61-64} sts.

Rows 3 thru {18-6}{13-6-8}: Continue to decrease one stitch at each edge in same manner, every row, {16-4}{11-4-6} times **more**: {14-41}{30-53-52} sts.

Size Small Only
Finish off.

Sizes Medium, Large, X-Large, and 2X-Large Only
Row {7}{14-7-9} (Decrease row): Ch 2, turn; skip next st, work across to last 3 sts, skip next 2 sts, hdc in last hdc: {38}{27-50-49} sts.

Row {8}{15-8-10} (Decrease row): Ch 2, turn; skip next st, work across to last 3 sts, skip next 2 sts, hdc in last hdc: {35}{24-47-46} sts.

Sizes Medium, X-Large Only, and 2X-Large Only
Rows 9 thru {18}{18-20}: Repeat Rows {7}{7-9} and {8}{8-10}, 5 times: {15}{14-16} sts.

Finish off.

Size Large Only
Rows 16-18: Repeat Rows 14 and 15 once, then repeat Row 14 once **more**: 15 sts.

Finish off.

FINISHING
With **right** sides together, whipstitch shoulder seams (*Fig. 6a, page 96*).

Sew in Sleeves, then sew underarm and side in one continuous seam.

EDGING
Row 1: With **right** side facing and working in end of rows, join yarn with slip st in Row 1 of Right Front; ch 2, dc in same row, work 104 dc evenly spaced across to marked row, work {35-36}{36-36-40} dc evenly spaced across to Back neck, work {20-22}{26-26-26} dc evenly spaced across Back neck, work {35-36}{36-36-40} dc evenly spaced across to marked row, work 105 dc across Left Front, hdc in same row as last dc: {302-306}{310-310-318} sts.

Row 2: Ch 2, turn; (work FPdc around each of next 2 dc, work BPdc around each of next 2 dc) across to last hdc, hdc in last hdc.

Row 3: Ch 2, turn; work BPdc around next BPdc, work FPdc around each of next 2 sts, (work BPdc around each of next 2 sts, work FPdc around each of next 2 sts) across to last 2 sts, work BPdc around next FPdc, hdc in last hdc.

Row 4: Ch 2, turn; (work BPdc around each of next 2 sts, work FPdc around each of next 2 sts) across to last hdc, hdc in last hdc.

Row 5: Ch 2, turn; work FPdc around next FPdc, work BPdc around each of next 2 sts, (work FPdc around each of next 2 sts, work BPdc around each of next 2 sts) across to last 2 sts, work FPdc around next BPdc, hdc in last hdc; finish off.

BELT

Ch 11.

Row 1: Dc in back ridge of third ch from hook and each ch across to last ch, hdc in last ch: 10 sts.

Row 2: Ch 2, turn; (work FPdc around each of next 2 sts, work BPdc around each of next 2 sts) twice, hdc in last st.

Row 3: Ch 2, turn; work BPdc around next BPdc, work FPdc around each of next 2 sts, work BPdc around each of next 2 sts, work FPdc around each of next 2 sts, work BPdc around next FPdc, hdc in last hdc.

Row 4: Ch 2, turn; (work BPdc around each of next 2 sts, work FPdc around each of next 2 sts) twice, hdc in last hdc.

Row 5: Ch 2, turn; work FPdc around next FPdc, work BPdc around each of next 2 sts, work FPdc around each of next 2 sts, work BPdc around each of next 2 sts, work FPdc around next BPdc, hdc in last hdc.

Repeat Rows 2-5 for pattern until Belt measures approximately 77" (195.5 cm) from beginning ch; finish off.

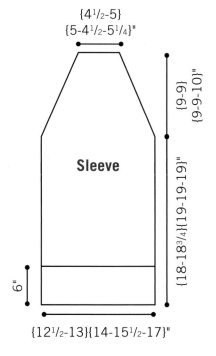

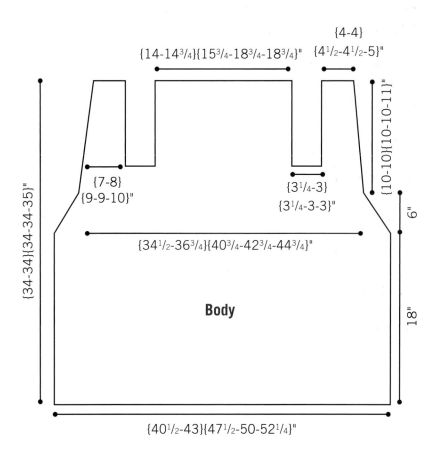

RUFFLED CARDIGAN

This versatile cardigan is crocheted with organic silk boucle making the stitches disappear creating a fabric with luxurious drape. And I love the ruffles you can make using post stitches!

■■■□ **INTERMEDIATE**

Size	Finished Chest Measurement
Small	33" (84 cm)
Medium	37" (94 cm)
Large	41" (104 cm)
X-Large	45" (114.5 cm)
2X-Large	49" (124.5 cm)

Size Note: Instructions are written with sizes Small and Medium in the first set of braces { } and sizes Large, X-Large, and 2X-Large in the second set of braces. Instructions will be easier to read if you circle all the numbers pertaining to your size. If only one number is given, it applies to all sizes.

MATERIALS

Medium Weight Yarn (4)
[1.75 ounces, 96 yards
(50 grams, 88 meters) per hank]:
  {6-7}{7-8-9} hanks
Crochet hook, size J (6 mm) **or** size needed
  for gauge
Yarn needle
Sewing needle and matching thread
Hook and eye

Photo model made using Plymouth Earth™ Collection Ecco Silk Boucle #100.

GAUGE: In pattern, 10 sts and 8 rows = 4" (10 cm)

Gauge Swatch: 4" (10 cm) square
Ch 11.
Row 1: Sc in second ch from hook, dc in next ch, (sc in next ch, dc in next ch) across: 10 sts.
Rows 2-8: Ch 1, turn; sc in first dc, dc in next sc, (sc in next dc, dc in next sc) across.
Finish off.

STITCH GUIDE
FRONT POST DOUBLE CROCHET
  (abbreviated FPdc)
YO, insert hook from **front** to **back** around post of st indicated *(Fig. 4, page 95)*, YO and pull up a loop (3 loops on hook), (YO and draw through 2 loops on hook) twice.

Instructions continued on page 16.

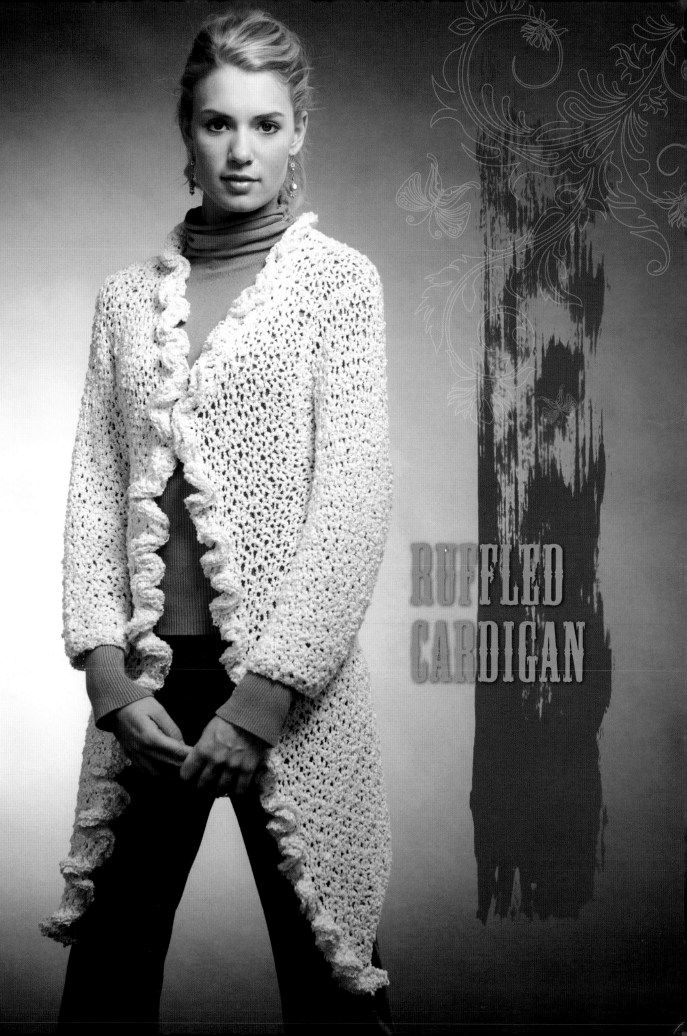

RUFFLED
CARDIGAN

Cardigan is worked in one piece to Armholes.

BODY

Ch {83-93}{103-113-123}.

Row 1 (Right side)**:** Sc in second ch from hook, dc in next ch, (sc in next ch, dc in next ch) across: {82-92}{102-112-122} sts.

Note: Loop a short piece of yarn around any stitch to mark Row 1 as **right** side.

Row 2: Ch 1, turn; sc in first dc, dc in next sc, (sc in next dc, dc in next sc) across.

Repeat Row 2 until Body measures approximately 21" (53.5 cm) from beginning ch, ending by working a **wrong** side row.

RIGHT FRONT

Sizes Small and X-Large Only
Row 1: Ch 1, turn; sc in first dc, dc in next sc, (sc in next dc, dc in next sc) {8}{13} times, leave remaining sts unworked: {18}{28} sts.

Row 2: Ch 1, turn; sc in first dc, dc in next sc, (sc in next dc, dc in next sc) across.

Repeat Row 2 until Right Front measures approximately 4¹/₂" (11.5 cm), ending by working a **right** side row.

Sizes Medium, Large, and 2X-Large Only
Row 1: Ch 1, turn; sc in first dc, (dc in next sc, sc in next dc) {10}{12-15} times, leave remaining sts unworked: {21}{25-31} sts.

Row 2: Ch 3 **(counts as first dc, now and throughout)**, turn; (sc in next dc, dc in next sc) across.

Row 3: Ch 1, turn; sc in first dc, (dc in next sc, sc in next dc) across.

Repeat Rows 2 and 3 until Right Front measures approximately 4¹/₂" (11.5 cm), ending by working Row 3.

NECK SHAPING

Size Small Only

Row 1 (Decrease row): Ch 1, turn; sc in first dc, (dc in next sc, sc in next dc) across to last sc, leave last sc unworked: 17 sts.

Row 2 (Decrease row): Ch 1, turn; skip first sc, (sc in next dc, dc in next sc) across: 16 sts.

Rows 3-9: Repeat Rows 1 and 2, 3 times; then repeat Row 1 once **more**: 9 sts.

Finish off.

Size X-Large Only

Row 1 (Decrease row): Ch 1, turn; sc in first dc, (dc in next sc, sc in next dc) across to last sc, leave last sc unworked: 27 sts.

Row 2: Ch 1, turn; skip first sc, (sc in next dc, dc in next sc) across: 26 sts.

Row 3: Repeat Row 1: 25 sts.

Row 4 (Decrease row): Turn; slip st in first 3 sts, ch 3 **(counts as first dc, now and throughout)**, (sc in next dc, dc in next sc) across: 23 sts.

Row 5 (Decrease row): Ch 1, turn; sc in first dc, (dc in next sc, sc in next dc) across to last 2 sts, leave last 2 sts unworked: 21 sts.

Rows 6-10: Repeat Rows 4 and 5 twice, then repeat Row 4 once **more**: 11 sts.

Finish off.

Sizes Medium, Large, and 2X-Large Only

Row 1: Ch 3, turn; sc in next dc, (dc in next sc, sc in next dc) across to last sc, leave last sc unworked: {20}{24-30} sts.

Row 2 (Decrease row): Ch 1, turn; skip first sc, sc in next dc, (dc in next sc, sc in next dc) across: {19}{23-29} sts.

Row 3 (Decrease row): Ch 3, turn; sc in next dc, (dc in next sc, sc in next dc) across to last sc, leave last sc unworked: {18}{22-28} sts.

Size Medium Only

Rows 4-6: Repeat Rows 2 and 3 once, then repeat Row 2 once **more**: 15 sts.

Row 7 (Decrease row): Ch 3, turn; (sc in next dc, dc in next sc) across to last 2 sts, leave last 2 sts unworked: 13 sts.

Row 8: Turn; slip st in first 2 sts, ch 1, sc in next dc, (dc in next sc, sc in next dc) across: 11 sts.

Row 9: Repeat Row 7: 9 sts.

Finish off.

Size Large Only

Rows 4 and 5: Repeat Rows 2 and 3: 20 sts.

Row 6 (Decrease row): Turn; slip st in first 3 sts, ch 3, sc in next dc, (dc in next sc, sc in next dc) across: 18 sts.

Row 7 (Decrease row): Ch 3, turn; sc in next dc, (dc in next sc, sc in next dc) across to last 2 sts, leave last 2 sts unworked: 16 sts.

Rows 8-10: Repeat Rows 6 and 7 once, then repeat Row 6 once **more**: 10 sts.

Finish off.

Size 2X-Large Only

Row 4 (Decrease row): Turn; slip st in first 3 sts, ch 3, sc in next dc, (dc in next sc, sc in next dc) across: 26 sts.

Row 5 (Decrease row): Ch 3, turn; sc in next dc, (dc in next sc, sc in next dc) across to last 2 sts, leave last 2 sts unworked: 24 sts.

Rows 6-11: Repeat Rows 4 and 5, 3 times: 12 sts.

Finish off.

Instructions continued on page 18.

BACK

Sizes Small, X-Large, and 2X-Large Only

Row 1: With **right** side facing, skip next {4}{6-7} sts from Right Front and join yarn with slip st in next dc; ch 1, sc in same st, dc in next sc, (sc in next dc, dc in next sc) {18}{21-22} times, leave remaining sts unworked: {38}{44-46} sts.

Row 2: Ch 1, turn; sc in first dc, dc in next sc, (sc in next dc, dc in next sc) across.

Repeat Row 2 for pattern until Back measures same as Right Front; finish off.

Sizes Medium and Large Only

Row 1: With **right** side facing, skip next 4 sts from Right Front and join yarn with slip st in next sc; ch 3, sc in next dc, (dc in next sc, sc in next dc) {20}{21} times, leave remaining sts unworked: {42}{44} sts.

Row 2: Ch 3, turn; sc in next dc, (dc in next sc, sc in next dc) across.

Repeat Row 2 for pattern until Back measures same as Right Front; finish off.

LEFT FRONT

Sizes Small and X-Large Only

Row 1: With **right** side facing, skip next {4}{6} sts from Back and join yarn with slip st in next dc; ch 1, sc in same st, dc in next sc, (sc in next dc, dc in next sc) across: {18}{28} sts.

Row 2: Ch 1, turn; sc in first dc, dc in next sc, (sc in next dc, dc in next sc) across.

Repeat Row 2 until Left Front measures approximately 4¹/₂" (11.5 cm), ending by working a **wrong** side row.

Sizes Medium, Large, and 2X-Large Only

Row 1: With **right** side facing, skip next {4}{4-7} sts from Back and join yarn with slip st in next sc; ch 3, (sc in next dc, dc in next sc) across: {21}{25-31} sts.

Row 2: Ch 1, turn; sc in first dc, (dc in next sc, sc in next dc) across.

Row 3: Ch 3, turn; (sc in next dc, dc in next sc) across.

Repeat Rows 2 and 3 until Left Front measures approximately 4¹/₂" (11.5 cm), ending by working Row 2.

NECK SHAPING
All Sizes

Complete same as Right Front.

SLEEVE (Make 2)

Ch 25.

Row 1 (Right side)**:** Sc in second ch from hook, dc in next ch, (sc in next ch, dc in next ch) across: 24 sts.

Note: Mark Row 1 as **right** side.

Row 2 (Increase row)**:** Ch 3, turn; sc in first dc, dc in next sc, (sc in next dc, dc in next sc) across: 25 sts.

Row 3 (Increase row)**:** Ch 3, turn; sc in first dc, (dc in next sc, sc in next dc) across: 26 sts.

Row 4 (Increase row)**:** Ch 1, turn; (sc, dc) in first sc, sc in next dc, (dc in next sc, sc in next dc) across: 27 sts.

Row 5 (Increase row)**:** Ch 1, turn; (sc, dc) in first sc, (sc in next dc, dc in next sc) across: 28 sts.

Repeat Rows 2-5, {4-4}{4-5-5} times; then repeat Row 2 once **more**: {45-45}{45-49-49} sts.

Sizes Large and 2X-Large Only

Repeat Rows 3 and 4 once **more**: {47-51} sts.

Work even until Sleeve measures approximately 15" (38 cm) from beginning ch; finish off.

FINISHING

Sew shoulder seams. Set in sleeves.

RUFFLE

Row 1: With **right** side facing, and working in ends of rows, join yarn with slip st in Row 1 of Right Front; ch 3, dc in same row, 2 dc in next row and in each row across, 2 dc in each st across Back neck edge, 2 dc in next row and in each row across.

Row 2: Ch 1, turn; 2 sc in each dc across.

Row 3: Ch 1, turn; working in **front** of sts on Row 2, work 2 FPdc around each dc on Row 1, slip st in last st on Row 2; finish off.

OPTIONAL BELT

Ch {127-137}{147-157-167}.

Row 1: 2 Dc in fourth ch from hook and in each ch across.

Row 2: Ch 1, turn; 2 sc in each st across.

Row 3: Ch 1, turn; working in **front** of sts on Row 2, work 2 FPdc around each dc on Row 1, slip st in last st on Row 2; finish off.

Using sewing needle and thread, sew hook and eye behind Ruffle at Neck Shaping. ✎

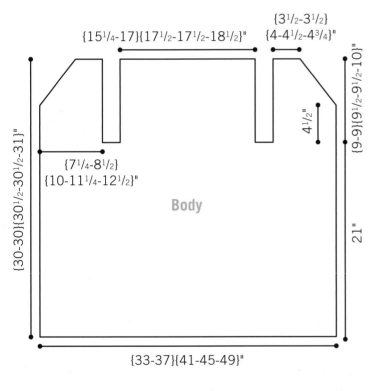

Body

{15¼-17}{17½-17½-18½}" {3½-3½}{4-4½-4¾}"

{7¼-8½}{10-11¼-12½}"

4½"

{9-9}{9½-9½-10}"

21"

{30-30}{30½-30½-31}"

{33-37}{41-45-49}"

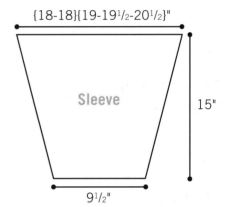

Sleeve

{18-18}{19-19½-20½}"

15"

9½"

PENCIL SKIRT

All over cabling creates amazing drape and a diamond pattern on this stylish skirt. Crocheted here in a luxurious angora-bamboo blend.

■■■□ INTERMEDIATE

Size	Finished Hip Measurement
Small	36" (91.5 cm)
Medium	40" (101.5 cm)
Large	42" (106.5 cm)
X-Large	46" (117 cm)
2X-Large	48" (122 cm)

Size Note: Instructions are written with sizes Small and Medium in the first set of braces { } and sizes Large, X-Large, and 2X-Large in the second set of braces. Instructions will be easier to read if you circle all the numbers pertaining to your size. If only one number is given, it applies to all sizes.

MATERIALS

Medium Weight Yarn 🔵**4**
[1.75 ounces, 80 yards
(50 grams, 73 meters) per ball]:
  {14-16}{17-19-20} balls
Crochet hook, size H (5 mm) **or** size needed
  for gauge
Yarn needle
Sewing needle and matching thread
³/₈" (10 mm) wide Elastic -
  cut to waist measurement
9" (23 cm) Zipper

Photo model made using Patons® Angora Bamboo #90018 Sienna Bronze.

GAUGE: In pattern,
    16 sts and 10 rows = 4" (10 cm)

Gauge Swatch: 4" (10 cm) square
Ch 18.
Row 1: Dc in fourth ch from hook **(3 skipped chs count as first dc)** and in each ch across: 16 dc.
Rows 2-10: Work same as Skirt, page 22.
Finish off.

STITCH GUIDE

FRONT POST DOUBLE CROCHET
    (abbreviated FPdc)
YO, insert hook from **front** to **back** around post of st indicated *(Fig. 4, page 95)*, YO and pull up a loop (3 loops on hook), (YO and draw through 2 loops on hook) twice.

BACK POST DOUBLE CROCHET
    (abbreviated BPdc)
YO, insert hook from **back** to **front** around post of st indicated *(Fig. 4, page 95)*, YO and pull up a loop (3 loops on hook), (YO and draw through 2 loops on hook) twice.

FP DECREASE (uses next 2 sts)
★ YO, insert hook from **front** to **back** around post of **next** st *(Fig. 4, page 95)*, YO and pull up a loop, YO and draw through 2 loops on hook; repeat from ★ once **more**, YO and draw through all 3 loops on hook.

Instructions continued on page 22.

PENCIL SKIRT

Skirt is worked from the waist down.

SKIRT

Ch {146-162}{170-186-194}.

Row 1: Dc in fourth ch from hook **(3 skipped chs count as first dc)** and in each ch across: {144-160}{168-184-192} dc.

Row 2 (Right side)**:** Ch 2 **(counts as first hdc, now and throughout)**, turn; work FPdc around each of next 2 dc, (work BPdc around each of next 2 dc, work FPdc around each of next 2 dc) across to last dc, hdc in last dc.

Note: Loop a short piece of yarn around any stitch to mark Row 2 as **right** side.

Row 3: Ch 2, turn; work BPdc around each of next 2 FPdc, (work FPdc around each of next 2 BPdc, work BPdc around each of next 2 FPdc) across to last hdc, hdc in last hdc.

Row 4: Ch 2, turn; work FPdc around next BPdc, ★ skip next BPdc, work BPdc around next FPdc, working in **front** of st just made, work FPdc around skipped BPdc, skip next FPdc, work FPdc around next BPdc, working **behind** st just made, work BPdc around skipped FPdc; repeat from ★ across to last 2 sts, work FPdc around next BPdc, hdc in last hdc.

Row 5: Ch 2, turn; work BPdc around next FPdc, work FPdc around next BPdc, work BPdc around each of next 2 FPdc, ★ work FPdc around each of next 2 BPdc, work BPdc around each of next 2 FPdc; repeat from ★ across to last 3 sts, work FPdc around next BPdc, work BPdc around next FPdc, hdc in last hdc.

Row 6: Ch 2, turn; work FPdc around next BPdc, BPdc around next FPdc, skip next BPdc, work FPdc around next BPdc, working in **front** of FPdc just made, work FPdc around skipped BPdc, ★ work BPdc around each of next 2 FPdc, skip next BPdc, work FPdc around next BPdc, working

in **front** of FPdc just made, work FPdc around skipped BPdc; repeat from ★ across to last 3 sts, work BPdc around next FPdc, work FPdc around next BPdc, hdc in last hdc.

Rows 7-9: Repeat Rows 5 and 6 once, then repeat Row 5 once **more**.

Row 10: Ch 2, turn; work FPdc around next BPdc, ★ skip next FPdc, work FPdc around next BPdc, working **behind** st just made, work BPdc around skipped FPdc, skip next BPdc, work BPdc around next FPdc, working in **front** of st just made, work FPdc around skipped BPdc; repeat from ★ across to last 2 sts, work FPdc around next BPdc, hdc in last hdc.

Row 11: Ch 2, turn; work BPdc around each of next 2 FPdc, (work FPdc around each of next 2 BPdc, work BPdc around each of next 2 FPdc) across to last st, hdc in last hdc.

Row 12: Ch 2, turn; work FPdc around each of next 2 BPdc, (work BPdc around each of next 2 FPdc, work FPdc around each of next 2 BPdc) across to last hdc, hdc in last hdc.

Row 13: Ch 2, turn; work BPdc around each of next 2 FPdc, (work FPdc around each of next 2 BPdc, work BPdc around each of next 2 FPdc) across to last hdc, hdc in last hdc.

Row 14: Ch 2, turn; skip next BPdc, work FPdc around next BPdc, working in **front** of st just made, work FPdc around skipped BPdc, ★ work BPdc around each of next 2 FPdc, skip next BPdc, work FPdc around next BPdc, working in **front** of st just made, work FPdc around skipped BPdc; repeat from ★ across to last hdc, hdc in last hdc.

Rows 15-17: Repeat Rows 13 and 14 once, then repeat Row 13 once **more**.

Row 18: Repeat Row 12.

Rows 19-32: Repeat Rows 3-16.

SHAPING

Row 1: Ch 2, turn; work BPdc around each of next 2 FPdc, work FP decrease, work BPdc around each of next 2 FPdc, ★ work FPdc around each of next 2 BPdc, work BPdc around each of next 2 FPdc, work FP decrease, work BPdc around each of next 2 FPdc; repeat from ★ across to last hdc, hdc in last hdc: {126-140}{147-161-168} sts.

Row 2: Ch 2, turn; work FPdc around each of next 2 BPdc, work BPdc around next FP decrease, work FPdc around each of next 2 BPdc, ★ work BPdc around each of next 2 FPdc, work FPdc around each of next 2 BPdc, work BPdc around next FP decrease, work FPdc around each of next 2 BPdc; repeat from ★ across to last hdc, hdc in last hdc.

Row 3: Ch 2, turn; work BPdc around each of next 2 FPdc, work FPdc around next BPdc, work BPdc around each of next 2 FPdc, ★ work FP decrease, work BPdc around each of next 2 FPdc, work FPdc around next BPdc, work BPdc around each of next 2 FPdc; repeat from ★ across to last hdc, hdc in last hdc: {109-121}{127-139-145} sts.

Row 4: Ch 2, turn; work FPdc around each of next 2 BPdc, (work BPdc around next st, work FPdc around each of next 2 BPdc) across to last hdc, hdc in last hdc.

Row 5: Ch 2, turn; work BPdc around each of next 2 FPdc, (work FPdc around next BPdc, work BPdc around each of next 2 FPdc) across to last hdc, hdc in last hdc.

Repeat Rows 4 and 5 until Skirt measures approximately 25" (63.5 cm) from beginning ch **or** to desired length, ending by working a **right** side row.

Finish off, leaving a long end for sewing.

FINISHING

Thread yarn needle with long end. With **right** side together, sew from bottom edge of Skirt to within 10" (25.5 cm) of top edge.

Aligning bottom of zipper to bottom of opening, sew in zipper.

Fold 1" (2.5 cm) of top edge of Skirt to **wrong** side and sew in place to create casing. Insert elastic, then sew open ends of casing closed, catching ends of elastic. ৡ

BUDAPEST NIGHTS

Inspired by the romantic bustling eastern European city, this full-length asymmetrical coat is the perfect combination of traditional and modern with the luxurious faux fur trim.

■■■■▶ **EXPERIENCED**

Size	Finished Chest Measurement
Small	39¹/₂" (100.5 cm)
Medium	47¹/₂" (120.5 cm)
Large	55¹/₂" (141 cm)
X-Large	63¹/₂" (161.5 cm)

Size Note: Instructions are written for size Small with sizes Medium, Large, and X-Large in braces { }. Instructions will be easier to read if you circle all the numbers pertaining to your size. If only one number is given, it applies to all sizes.

MATERIALS

Medium Weight Yarn 🔲**4**
[3 ounces, 185 yards
(85 grams, 170 meters) per skein]:
  22{26-29-32} skeins
Crochet hook, size H (5 mm) **or** size needed
  for gauge
Split-ring markers - 2
Yarn needle
Sewing needle and matching thread
Straight pins
1³/₄" (44 mm) Buttons - 6
³/₄" (19 mm) Buttons - 4
Faux fur - approximately ³/₄ yard (.75 meter)

Photo model made using Naturally Caron® Country #0017 Claret.

GAUGE: In pattern,
    16 sts and 10 rows = 4" (10 cm)

Gauge Swatch: 4" (10 cm) square
Ch 17.
Row 1: Sc in second ch from hook and in each ch across: 16 sc.
Row 2: Ch 3 **(counts as first dc)**, turn; dc in next sc and in each sc across.
Row 3: Ch 1, turn; sc in each dc across.
Rows 4-10: Repeat Rows 2 and 3, 3 times; then repeat Row 2 once **more**.
Finish off.

Instructions continued on page 26.

BUDAPEST
NIGHTS

STITCH GUIDE

BOBBLE

Insert hook in next st, YO and pull up a loop, (YO and draw through one loop) 3 times, YO and draw both loops on hook. Push Bobble to **right** side.

BACK POST TREBLE CROCHET
(abbreviated BPtr)

Working **behind** previous row, YO twice, insert hook from **back** to **front** around post of st indicated 2 rows **below** *(Fig. 4, page 95)*, YO and pull up a loop (4 loops on hook), (YO and draw through 2 loops on hook) 3 times. Skip st in front of BPtr.

FRONT POST TREBLE CROCHET
(abbreviated FPtr)

Working in **front** of previous row, YO twice, insert hook from **front** to **back** around post of st indicated 2 rows **below** *(Fig. 4, page 95)*, YO and pull up a loop (4 loops on hook), (YO and draw through 2 loops on hook) 3 times. Skip st behind FPtr.

SPLIT FRONT POST TREBLE
(abbreviated Split FPtr)

First Leg: Working in **front** of previous rows, YO twice, insert hook from **front** to **back** around post of st indicated 2 rows **below** *(Fig. 4, page 95)*, YO and pull up a loop (4 loops on hook), (YO and draw through 2 loops) twice.

Second Leg: YO twice, insert hook from **front** to **back** around post of st indicated 2 rows **below**, YO and pull up a loop (5 loops on hoo), (YO and draw through 2 loops) twice, YO and draw through all 3 loops on hook. Skip st behind Split FPtr.

DOUBLE CROCHET DECREASE
(abbreviated dc decrease) (uses next 2 sts)

★ YO, insert hook in **next** st, YO and pull up a loop, YO and draw through 2 loops on hook; repeat from ★ once **more**, YO and draw through all 3 loops on hook (**counts as one dc**).

CENTER PANEL

Begin and end in marked stitches for each row.

Row 1 (Right side): Sc in next 3 sc, (work Bobble, sc in next 3 sc) across.

Row 2: Dc in each st across.

Row 3: Sc in next dc, work Bobble, sc in next dc, work First Leg of Split FPtr around st 2 rows **below** last Bobble made, skip next 3 sts, work Second Leg around next st, sc in next dc on previous row, work Bobble, sc in next dc, ★ work First Leg of Split FPtr around same st as Second Leg of last Split FPtr made, skip next 3 sts, work Second Leg around next st, sc in next dc on previous row, work Bobble, sc in next dc; repeat from ★ across.

Row 4: Dc in each st across.

Row 5: Sc in next dc, work FPtr around first Split FPtr 2 rows **below**, sc in next dc on previous row, work Bobble, sc in next dc, ★ work First Leg of Split FPtr around same Split FPtr just worked around, skip next 3 sts, work Second Leg around next st, sc in next dc on previous row, work Bobble, sc in next dc; repeat from ★ across to last 2 sts, work FPtr around same st as Second Leg of last Split FPtr made, sc in last dc.

Repeat Rows 2-5 for pattern.

BACK

Ch 106{122-138-154}.

Row 1: Sc in second ch from hook and in next 23{31-35-39} chs, place split-ring marker around last sc made to mark first st of Center Panel, sc in next 58{58-66-74} chs, place split-ring marker around last sc made to mark last st of Center Panel, sc in each ch across: 105{121-137-153} sc.

Move markers up after each row is completed.

Row 2 (Right side)**:** Ch 1, turn; sc in each sc across to first marker, work Row 1 of Center Panel, sc in each sc across.

Note: Loop a short piece of yarn around any stitch to mark Row 2 as **right** side.

Row 3: Ch 3 **(counts as first dc, now and throughout)**, turn; dc in next sc and in each st across.

Row 4: Ch 1, turn; sc in each st across to first marker, work Row 3 of Center Panel, sc in each st across.

Row 5: Ch 3, turn; working around sts 2 rows **below**, (work FPtr around next st, work BPtr around next st) across to first marker, work Row 4 of Center Panel, (work BPtr around next st, work FPtr around next st) across to last sc on previous row, dc in last sc.

Row 6: Ch 1, turn; sc in each st across to first marker, work Row 5 of Center Panel, sc in each st across.

Row 7: Ch 3, turn; (work FPtr around next FPtr, work BPtr around next BPtr) across to first marker, work Row 2 of Center Panel, (work BPtr around next BPtr, work FPtr around next FPtr) across to last sc on previous row, dc in last sc.

Row 8: Ch 1, turn; sc in each st across to first marker, work Row 3 of Center Panel, sc in each st across.

Maintain established pattern on each side of Center Panel. On **wrong** side rows, work FPtr around FPtr and work BPtr around BPtr throughout.

Row 9 (Decrease row)**:** Turn; slip st in first 2 sc, ch 3, work across to first marker, work Row 4 of Center Panel, work across to last sc on previous row, dc in last sc: 104{120-136-152} sts.

Instructions continued on page 28.

Row 10: Ch 1, turn; sc in each st across to first marker, work Row 5 of Center Panel, sc in each st across.

Row 11 (Decrease row): Ch 3, turn; work across to first marker, work Row 2 of Center Panel, work across to last 2 sts, dc decrease: 103{119-135-151} sts.

Rows 12-59: Repeat Rows 8-11, 12 times: 79{95-111-127} sts.

Rows 60-91: Repeat Rows 4-7, 8 times; do **not** finish off.

ARMHOLE SHAPING
Size Small Only
Row 1: Turn; slip st in first 9 sts, ch 1, sc in same st and in next st, work Row 3 of Center Panel, sc in next 2 sts, leave remaining 8 sts unworked: 63 sts.

Rows 2-23: Work even.

Finish off.

Sizes Medium, Large, and X-Large Only
Row 1: Turn; slip st in first {9-7-9} sts, ch 1, sc in same st and in each st across to first marker, work Row 3 of Center Panel, sc in each st across to last {8-6-8} sts, leave remaining sts unworked: {79-99-111} sts.

Row 2: Turn; slip st in first {9-8-9} sts, ch 3, work across to first marker, work Row 4 of Center Panel, work across to last {8-7-8} sts, leave remaining sts unworked: {63-85-95} sts.

Size Medium Only
Rows 3-23: Work even.

Finish off.

Sizes Large and X-Large Only
Row 3: Turn; slip st in first {8-9} sts, ch 1, sc in same st and in next st, work Row 5 of Center Panel, sc in next 2 sts, leave remaining {7-8} sts unworked: {71-79} sts.

Rows 4-25: Work even.

Finish off.

RIGHT FRONT
Ch 77{89-101-109}.

Row 1: Sc in second ch from hook and in next 23{31-35-39} chs, place marker around last sc made, sc in each ch across to last 2 chs, place marker around last sc made, sc in last 2 chs: 76{88-100-108} sc.

Row 2 (Right side): Ch 1, turn; sc in first 2 sc, work Row 1 of Center Pattern, sc in each sc across.

Note: Mark Row 2 as **right** side.

Row 3: Ch 3, turn; dc in next sc and in each st across.

Row 4: Ch 1, turn; sc in first 2 sts, work Row 3 of Center Panel, sc in each st across.

Row 5: Ch 3, turn; working around sts 2 rows **below**, (work FPtr around next st, work BPtr around next st) across to first marker, work Row 4 of Center Panel, work BPtr around next st, dc in last sc on previous row.

Row 6: Ch 1, turn; sc in first 2 sts, work Row 5 of Center Panel, sc in each st across.

Row 7: Ch 3, turn; (work FPtr around next FPtr, work BPtr around next BPtr) across to first marker, work Row 2 of Center Panel, work BPtr around next BPtr, dc in last sc on previous row.

Row 8: Ch 1, turn; sc in first 2 sts, work Row 3 of Center Panel, sc in each st across.

Maintain established pattern on each side of Center Panel. On **wrong** side rows, work FPtr around FPtr and work BPtr around BPtr throughout.

Row 9 (Decrease row)**:** Turn; slip st in first 2 sc, ch 3, work across to first marker, work Row 4 of Center Panel, work BPtr around next BPtr, dc in last sc on previous row: 75{87-99-107} sts.

Row 10: Ch 1, turn; sc in first 2 sts, work Row 5 of Center Panel, sc in each st across.

Row 11: Ch 3, turn; work across to first marker, work Row 2 of Center Panel, work BPtr around next BPtr, dc in last sc on previous row

Row 12: Ch 1, turn; sc in first 2 sts, work Row 3 of Center Panel, sc in each st across.

Row 13 (Decrease row)**:** Turn; slip st in first 2 sc, ch 3, work across to first marker, work Row 4 of Center Panel, work BPtr around next BPtr, dc in last sc on previous row: 74{86-98-106} sts.

Row 14: Ch 1, turn; sc in first 2 sts, work Row 5 of Center Panel, work BPtr around next BPtr, dc in last sc on previous row.

Rows 16-59: Repeat Rows 8-15, 5 times; then repeat Rows 8-11 once **more**: 63{75-87-95} sts.

Rows 60-91: Repeat Rows 4-7, 8 times; do **not** finish off.

ARMHOLE AND NECK SHAPING
Size Small Only
Row 1: Ch 1, turn; sc in first 2 sts, work Row 3 of Center Panel, sc in each st across to last 8 sts, leave remaining sts unworked: 55 sts.

Rows 2-15: Work even; do **not** finish off.

Sizes Medium, Large, and X-Large Only
Row 1: Ch 1, turn; sc in first 2 sts, work Row 3 of Center Panel, sc in each st across to last {8-6-8} sts, leave remaining sts unworked: {67-81-87} sts.

Row 2: Turn; slip st in first {9-8-9} sts, ch 3, work across to first marker, work Row 4 of Center Panel, work BPtr around next BPtr, dc in last sc on previous row: {59-74-79} sts.

Size Medium Only
Rows 3-15: Work even; do **not** finish off.

Sizes Large and X-Large Only
Row 3: Ch 1, turn; sc in first 2 sts, work Row 5 of Center Panel, sc in each st across to last {7-8} sts, leave remaining sts unworked: {67-71} sts.

Rows 4-15: Work even; do **not** finish off.

Instructions continued on page 30.

Row 16 (Decrease row): Ch 3, turn; work across to first marker, work Row 2 of Center Panel across to last 10 sts, dc decrease 4 times, work BPtr around next BPtr, dc in last sc on previous row: 51{55-63-67} sts.

Row 17: Ch 1, turn; sc in first 6 sts, work Row 3 of Center Panel, sc in last 2 sts.

Row 18 (Decrease row): Ch 3, turn; work BPtr around next BPtr, work Row 4 of Center Panel across to last 10 sts, dc decrease 4 times, work BPtr around next BPtr, dc in last sc on previous row: 47{51-59-63} sts.

Row 19: Ch 1, turn; sc in first 6 sts, work Row 5 of Center Panel, sc in last 2 sts.

Rows 20 thru 23{23-25-25}: Repeat Rows 16-19 once, then repeat Rows 16 and 17 0{0-1-1} time(s) **more**: 39{43-47-51} sts.

Finish off.

Place marker around last dc on Row 16 for Collar placement.

LEFT FRONT

Ch 77{89-101-109}.

Row 1: Sc in second ch from hook and in each ch across: 76{88-100-108} sc.

Row 2 (Right side): Ch 1, turn; sc in each sc across.

Note: Mark Row 2 as **right** side.

Row 3: Ch 3, turn; dc in next sc and in each sc across.

Row 4: Ch 1, turn; sc in each dc across.

Row 5: Ch 3, turn; work BPtr around next dc, dc in next 51{55-63-67} sc, place marker around last sc made, (work BPtr around next dc, work FPtr around next dc) across to last sc on previous row, dc in last sc.

Row 6: Ch 1, turn; sc in each st across.

Row 7: Ch 3, turn; work BPtr around next BPtr, dc in next sc and in each sc across to marker (working in marked sc), (work BPtr around next BPtr, work FPtr around next FPtr) across to last sc on previous row, dc in last sc.

Row 8: Ch 1, turn; sc in each st across.

Row 9 (Decrease row): Ch 3, turn; work BPtr around next BPtr, dc in next sc and in each sc across to marker, work BPtr around next BPtr, (work FPtr around next FPtr, work BPtr around next BPtr) across to last 2 sc on previous row, dc decrease: 75{87-99-107} sts.

Row 10: Ch 1, turn; sc in each st across.

Row 11: Ch 3, turn; work BPtr around next BPtr, dc in next sc and in each sc across to marker, work BPtr around next BPtr, (work FPtr around next FPtr, work BPtr around next BPtr) across to last sc on previous row, dc in last sc.

Row 12: Ch 1, turn; sc in each st across.

Row 13 (Decrease row)**:** Ch 3, turn; work BPtr around next BPtr, dc in next sc and in each sc across to marker, (work BPtr around next BPtr, work FPtr around next FPtr) across to last 2 sc on previous row, dc decrease: 74{86-98-106} sts.

Row 14: Ch 1, turn; sc in each st across.

Row 15: Ch 3, turn; work BPtr around next BPtr, dc in next sc and in each sc across to marker, (work BPtr around next BPtr, work FPtr around next FPtr) across to last sc on previous row, dc in last sc.

Rows 16-57: Repeat Rows 8-15, 5 times; then repeat Rows 8 and 9 once **more**: 63{75-87-95} sts.

Rows 58-91: Repeat Rows 10 and 11, 17 times; do **not** finish off.

ARMHOLE AND NECK SHAPING
Size Small Only
Row 1: Turn; slip st in first 9 sts, ch 1, sc in same st and in each st across: 55 sts.

Rows 2-15: Work even; do **not** finish off.

Sizes Medium, Large, and X-Large Only
Row 1: Turn; slip st in first {9-7-9} sts, ch 1, sc in same st and in each st across: {67-81-87} sc.

Row 2: Ch 3, turn; work BPtr around next BPtr, dc in next sc and in each sc across to marker, work across to last {9-8-9} sc on previous row, dc in next sc, leave remaining sts unworked: {59-74-79} sts.

Size Medium Only
Rows 3-15: Work even; do **not** finish off.

Sizes Large and X-Large Only
Row 3: Turn; slip st in first {8-9} sts, ch 1, sc in same st and in each st across: {67-71} sc.

Rows 4-15: Work even; do **not** finish off.

All Sizes
Row 16 (Decrease row)**:** Ch 3, turn; work BPtr around next BPtr, dc decrease 4 times, dc in next sc and in each sc across to marker, (work BPtr around next BPtr, work FPtr around next FPtr) across to last sc on previous row, dc in last sc: 51{51-63-67} sts.

Row 17: Ch 1, turn; sc in each st across.

Rows 18 thru 23{23-25-25}: Repeat Rows 16 and 17, 3{3-4-4} times: 39{43-47-51} sts.

Finish off.

Place marker around first dc on Row 16 for Collar placement.

Instructions continued on page 32.

Row 4: Ch 1, turn; sc in each st across to first marker, work Row 3 of Center Panel, sc in each st across.

Sizes Small and Medium Only

Row 5: Ch 3, turn; work FPtr around next dc, work BPtr around next dc, work FPtr around next dc, work Row 4 of Center Panel, work FPtr around next dc, work BPtr around next dc, work FPtr around next dc, dc in last sc on previous row.

Row 6: Ch 1, turn; sc in each st across to first marker, work Row 5 of Center Panel, sc in each st across.

Row 7: Ch 3, turn; work FPtr around next FPtr, work BPtr around next BPtr, work FPtr around next FPtr, work Row 2 of Center Panel, work FPtr around next FPtr, work BPtr around next BPtr, work FPtr around next FPtr, dc in last sc on previous row.

Row 8: Ch 1, turn; sc in each st across to first marker, work Row 3 of Center Panel, sc in each st across.

Row 9: Ch 3, turn; work FPtr around next FPtr, work BPtr around next BPtr, work FPtr around next FPtr, work Row 4 of Center Panel, work FPtr around next FPtr, work BPtr around next BPtr, work FPtr around next FPtr, dc in last sc on previous row.

Row 10: Ch 1, turn; sc in each st across to first marker, work Row 5 of Center Panel, sc in each st across.

Row 11 (Increase row): Ch 3, turn; dc in next sc, work FPtr around first FPtr, work BPtr around next BPtr, work FPtr around next FPtr, work Row 2 of Center Panel, work FPtr around next FPtr, work BPtr around next BPtr, work FPtr around next FPtr, dc in last 2 sc on previous row: 53 sts.

Row 12: Ch 1, turn; sc in each st across to first marker, work Row 3 of Center Panel, sc in each st across.

Row 13: Ch 3, turn; (work BPtr around next st, work FPtr around next FPtr) twice, work Row 4 of Center Panel, (work FPtr around next FPtr, work BPtr around next st) twice, dc in last sc on previous row.

SLEEVE (Make 2)
Ch 52{52-56-56}.

Row 1: Sc in second ch from hook and in next 4{4-6-6} chs, place marker around last sc made, sc in next 42 chs, place marker around last sc made, sc in last 4{4-6-6} chs: 51{51-55-55} sc.

Row 2 (Right side): Ch 1, turn; sc in each sc across to first marker, work Row 1 of Center Panel, sc in each sc across.

Note: Mark Row 2 as **right** side.

Row 3: Ch 3, turn; dc in next sc and in each st across.

Row 14: Ch 1, turn; sc in each st across to first marker, work Row 5 of Center Panel, sc in each st across.

Row 15 (Increase row): Ch 3, turn; dc in next sc, work BPtr around first BPtr, work FPtr around next FPtr, work BPtr around next BPtr, work FPtr around next FPtr, work Row 2 of Center Panel, (work FPtr around next FPtr, work BPtr around next BPtr) twice, dc in last 2 sc on previous row: 55 sts.

Sizes Large and X-Large Only
Row 5: Ch 3, turn; work FPtr around next dc, (work BPtr around next dc, work FPtr around next dc) twice, work Row 4 of Center Panel, work FPtr around next dc, (work BPtr around next dc, work FPtr around next dc) twice, dc in last sc on previous row.

Row 6: Ch 1, turn; sc in each st across to first marker, work Row 5 of Center Panel, sc in each st across.

Row 7: Ch 3, turn; work FPtr around next FPtr, (work BPtr around next BPtr, work FPtr around next FPtr) twice, work Row 2 of Center Panel, work FPtr around next FPtr, (work BPtr around next BPtr, work FPtr around next FPtr) twice, dc in last sc on previous row.

Row 8: Ch 1, turn; sc in each st across to first marker, work Row 3 of Center Panel, sc in each st across.

Row 9: Ch 3, turn; work FPtr around next FPtr, (work BPtr around next BPtr, work FPtr around next FPtr) twice, work Row 4 of Center Panel, work FPtr around next FPtr, (work BPtr around next BPtr, work FPtr around next FPtr) twice, dc in last sc on previous row.

Row 10: Ch 1, turn; sc in each st across to first marker, work Row 5 of Center Panel, sc in each st across.

Row 11 (Increase row): Ch 3, turn; dc in next sc, work FPtr around first FPtr, (work BPtr around next BPtr, work FPtr around next FPtr) twice, work Row 2 of Center Panel, work FPtr around next FPtr, (work BPtr around next BPtr, work FPtr around next FPtr) twice, dc in last 2 sc on previous row: 57 sts.

Row 12: Ch 1, turn; sc in each st across to first marker, work Row 3 of Center Panel, sc in each st across.

Row 13: Ch 3, turn; work BPtr around next dc, work across to first marker, work Row 4 of Center Panel, work across to last 2 sts, work BPtr around next dc, dc in last sc on previous row.

Row 14: Ch 1, turn; sc in each st across to first marker, work Row 5 of Center Panel, sc in each st across.

Row 15 (Increase row): Ch 3, turn; dc in next sc, work BPtr around first BPtr, work across to first marker, work Row 2 of Center Panel, work across to last 2 sc on previous row, dc in last 2 sc on previous row: 59 sts.

All Sizes
Row 16: Ch 1, turn; sc in each st across to first marker, work Row 3 of Center Panel, sc in each st across.

Row 17: Ch 3, turn; work FPtr around next dc, work across to first marker, work Row 4 of Center Panel, work across to last 2 sts, work FPtr around next dc, dc in last sc on previous row.

Instructions continued on page 34.

Row 18: Ch 1, turn; sc in each st across to first marker, work Row 5 of Center Panel, sc in each st across.

Row 19 (Increase row)**:** Ch 3, turn; dc in next sc, work FPtr around first FPtr, work across to first marker, work Row 2 of Center Panel, work across to last 2 sc on previous row, dc in last 2 sc: 57{57-61-61} sts.

Row 20: Ch 1, turn; sc in each st across to first marker, work Row 3 of Center Panel, sc in each st across.

Row 21: Ch 3, turn; work BPtr around next dc, work across to first marker, work Row 4 of Center Panel, work across to last 2 sts, work BPtr around next dc, dc in last sc on previous row.

Row 22: Ch 1, turn; sc in each st across to first marker, work Row 5 of Center Panel, sc in each st across.

Row 23 (Increase row)**:** Ch 3, turn; dc in next sc, work BPtr around first BPtr, work across to first marker, work Row 2 of Center Panel, work across to last 2 sc on previous row, dc in last 2 sc: 59{59-63-63} sts.

Rows 24-47: Repeat Rows 16-23, 3 times: 71{71-75-75} sts.

Rows 48-52: Work even.

Finish off.

FINISHING

With **right** sides together, sew shoulder seams across first 17{20-22-24} sts. Sew in sleeves.

Sew underarm and side in one continuous seam.

COLLAR

Row 1: With **right** side facing, join yarn with sc in marked dc on Right Front **(see Joining With Sc, page 94)**; working in end of rows and in sts acros Neck edge, sc in each st across to marked dc on Left Front.

Row 2: Ch 3, turn; dc in next sc and in each sc across.

Row 3: Ch 1, turn; sc in each dc across.

Rows 4-9: Repeat Rows 2 and 3, 3 times.

Finish off.

Measure bottom edge of Coat and Sleeves. Cut faux fur 8" (20.5 cm) wide and to length. Pin fur pieces in place, folding over to enclose edges of Coat and Sleeves. With sewing needle and thread, carefully hand-stitch in place.

Using photo, page 25, as a guide for placement, sew 6 large buttons to Left Front, evenly spaced across. Sew remaining 4 smaller buttons to **wrong** side of Right Front, placing first button 2" (5 cm) up from beginning of Armhole and spacing remaining 3 buttons 7" (18 cm) apart below first button. Use spaces in end of rows along Left Front as buttonholes.

BUTTON LOOPS (Make 4)

Ch 10; join with slip st to form a ring; finish off leaving a long end for sewing.

Sew Button Loops to **wrong** side of Right Front opposite top 4 large buttons. ✎

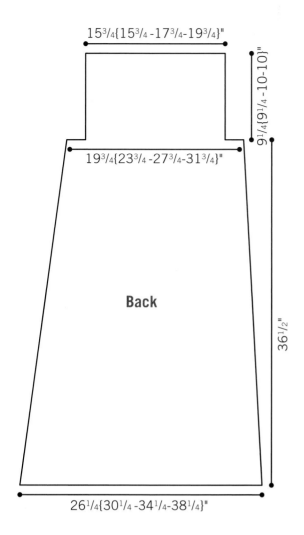

15³/₄{15³/₄-17³/₄-19³/₄}"

9¹/₄{9¹/₄-10-10}"

19³/₄{23³/₄-27³/₄-31³/₄}"

Back

36¹/₂"

26¹/₄{30¹/₄-34¹/₄-38¹/₄}"

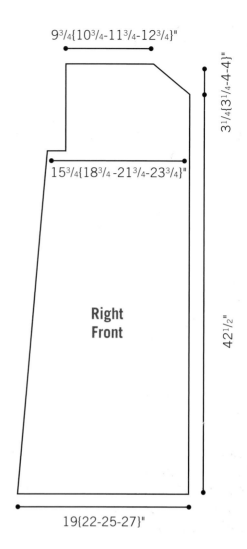

9³/₄{10³/₄-11³/₄-12³/₄}"

3¹/₄{3¹/₄-4-4}"

15³/₄{18³/₄-21³/₄-23³/₄}"

Right Front

42¹/₂"

19{22-25-27}"

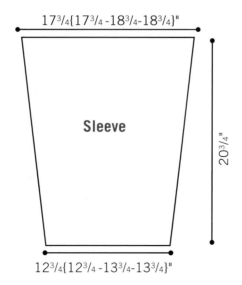

17³/₄{17³/₄-18³/₄-18³/₄}"

Sleeve

20³/₄"

12³/₄{12³/₄-13³/₄-13³/₄}"

ANTEBELLUM

The baby doll has been around since the 1950s and as it continues to grow in popularity, you can find many variations of this cute style. Here is my crocheted version using post stitches to emphasize the shape and texture.

■■■□ INTERMEDIATE

Size	Finished Chest Measurement
Small	32" (81.5 cm)
Medium	36" (91.5 cm)
Large	40" (101.5 cm)
X-Large	44" (112 cm)
2X-Large	48" (122 cm)

Size Note: Instructions are written with sizes Small and Medium in the first set of braces { } and sizes Large, X-Large, and 2X-Large in the second set of braces. Instructions will be easier to read if you circle all the numbers pertaining to your size. If only one number is given, it applies to all sizes.

MATERIALS

Light Weight Yarn **(3)**
[3.5 ounces, 403 yards
(100 grams, 369 meters) per skein]:
   {6-6}{7-8-9} skeins
Crochet hook, size F (3.75 mm) **or** size needed
   for gauge
Yarn needle

Photo model made using Plymouth Yarn® Bungee #24.

GAUGES: In Ribbing pattern,
22 sts and 8 rows = 4" (10 cm)
In lower Bodice pattern,
17 sts and 8 rows = 4" (10 cm)
In upper Bodice pattern,
(V-st, FPdc) 6 times and 12 rows = 4" (10 cm)

Gauge Swatch: 4" (10 cm) square
Ch 21.
Row 1: Dc in fourth ch from hook and in each ch across: 19 sts.
Rows 2-8: Work same as Bodice, page 38.
Finish off.

Instructions continued on page 38.

ANTEBELLUM

STITCH GUIDE

FRONT POST DOUBLE CROCHET
(abbreviated FPdc)
YO, insert hook from **front** to **back** around post of st indicated *(Fig. 4, page 95)*, YO and pull up a loop (3 loops on hook), (YO and draw through 2 loops on hook) twice.

BACK POST DOUBLE CROCHET
(abbreviated BPdc)
YO, insert hook from **back** to **front** around post of st indicated *(Fig. 4, page 95)*, YO and pull up a loop (3 loops on hook), (YO and draw through 2 loops on hook) twice.

V-STITCH *(abbreviated V-St)*
(Dc, ch 1, dc) in st or sp indicated.

DECREASE (uses next 3 sts)
† YO, insert hook from **front** to **back** around post of **next** BPdc *(Fig. 4, page 95)*, YO and pull up a loop, YO and draw through 2 loops on hook †, skip next V-St, repeat from † to † once, YO and draw through all 3 loops on hook **(counts as one FPdc)**.

BACK
BODICE

Ch {73-85}{97-111-123}, place marker around third ch from hook for st placement.

Row 1 (Wrong side)**:** Dc in back ridge of fourth ch from hook and each ch across *(Fig. 1, page 95)*: {71-83}{95-109-121} sts.

Note: Loop a short piece of yarn around the **back** of any stitch on Row 1 to mark **right** side.

Row 2: Ch 2 **(counts as first hdc, now and throughout)**, turn; (work FPdc around next st, hdc in next st) across.

Row 3: Ch 2, turn; (work BPdc around next FPdc, hdc in next hdc) across.

Rows 4-9: Repeat Rows 2 and 3, 3 times.

ARMHOLE SHAPING

Row 1: Turn; slip st in first {7-7}{9-9-11} sts, ch 2, work FPdc around next BPdc, (work V-St in next hdc, work FPdc around next BPdc) across to last {7-7}{9-9-11} sts, hdc in next hdc, leave remaining sts unworked: {28-34}{38-45-49} V-Sts.

Row 2: Ch 2, turn; work BPdc around next FPdc, ★ work V-St in next V-St (ch-1 sp), work BPdc around next FPdc; repeat from ★ across to last hdc, hdc in last hdc.

Row 3 (Decrease row)**:** Ch 2, turn; decrease, work V-St in next V-St, (work FPdc around next BPdc, work V-St in next V-St) across to last 2 BPdc, decrease, hdc in last hdc: {26-32}{36-43-47} V-Sts.

Row 4: Ch 2, turn; work BPdc around next FPdc, (work V-St in next V-St, work BPdc around next FPdc) across to last hdc, hdc in last hdc.

Rows 5 thru {12-16}{18-22-26}: Repeat Rows 3 and 4, {4-6}{7-9-11} times: {18-20}{22-25-25} V-Sts.

Work even until Armholes measure approximately {8-8}{8¹/₂-8¹/₂-9}"/{20.5-20.5}{21.5-21.5-23} cm, ending by working a **wrong** side row.

Finish off.

RIBBING

Row 1: With **right** side facing and working in free loops of beginning ch *(Fig. 3, page 95)*, join yarn with slip st in marked ch; ch 2, work FPdc around next dc, (work BPdc around next dc, work FPdc around next dc) across to last ch, hdc in last ch: {71-83}{95-109-121} sts.

Row 2: Ch 2, turn; work BPdc around next FPdc, (work FPdc around next BPdc, work BPdc around next FPdc) across to last hdc, hdc in last hdc.

Row 3: Ch 2, turn; work FPdc around next BPdc, (work BPdc around next FPdc, work FPdc around next BPdc) across to last hdc, hdc in last hdc.

Rows 4-6: Repeat Rows 2 and 3 once, then repeat Row 2 once **more**; do **not** finish off.

If you would like a longer length to the Waist Ribbing, you can continue to repeat Rows 2 and 3 as many times as you'd like, just be sure to end by working Row 2.

SKIRT

Row 1: Ch 2, turn; work FPdc around next BPdc, (work V-St in next FPdc, work FPdc around next BPdc) across to last hdc, hdc in last hdc: {34-40}{46-53-59} V-Sts.

Row 2: Ch 2, turn; work BPdc around next FPdc, (work V-St in next V-st, work BPdc around next FPdc) across to last hdc, hdc in last hdc.

Row 3: Ch 2, turn; work FPdc around next BPdc, (work V-St in next V-St, work FPdc around next BPdc) across to last hdc, hdc in last hdc.

Rows 4-10: Repeat Rows 2 and 3, 3 times; then repeat Row 2 once **more**.

Row 11: Ch 2, turn; work FPdc around next BPdc, ★ (2 dc, ch 1, dc) in next V-St, work FPdc around next BPdc; repeat from ★ across to last hdc, hdc in last hdc.

Row 12: Ch 2, turn; work BPdc around next FPdc, ★ (2 dc, ch 1, dc) in next ch-1 sp, work BPdc around next FPdc; repeat from ★ across to last hdc, hdc in last hdc.

Row 13: Ch 2, turn; work FPdc around next BPdc, ★ (2 dc, ch 1, dc) in next ch-1 sp, work FPdc around next BPdc; repeat from ★ across to last hdc, hdc in last hdc.

Rows 14-20: Repeat Rows 12 and 13, 3 times; then repeat Row 12 once **more**.

Row 21: Ch 2, turn; work FPdc around next BPdc, ★ (2 dc, ch 1, 2 dc) in next ch-1 sp, work FPdc around next BPdc; repeat from ★ across to last hdc, hdc in last hdc.

Row 22: Ch 2, turn; work BPdc around next FPdc, ★ (2 dc, ch 1, 2 dc) in next ch-1 sp, work BPdc around next FPdc; repeat from ★ across to last hdc, hdc in last hdc.

Rows 23-30: Repeat Rows 21 and 22, 4 times.

Row 31: Ch 2, turn; work FPdc around next BPdc, ★ 6 dc in next ch-1 sp, work FPdc around next BPdc; repeat from ★ across to last hdc, hdc in last hdc, finish off.

FRONT
BODICE

Work same as Back to Armhole Shaping: {71-83}{95-109-121} sts.

LEFT FRONT NECK AND ARMHOLE SHAPING

Row 1: Turn; slip st in first {7-7}{9-9-11} sts, ch 2, work FPdc around next BPdc, (work V-St in next hdc, work FPdc around next BPdc) {12-15}{17-20-22} times, hdc in next hdc, leave remaining {38-44}{50-58-64} sts unworked: {12-15}{17-20-22} V-Sts.

Row 2: Ch 2, turn; work BPdc around next FPdc, (work V-St in next V-St, work BPdc around next FPdc) across to last hdc, hdc in last hdc.

Instructions continued on page 40.

Row 3 (Decrease row): Ch 2, turn; decrease, (work V-St in next V-St, work FPdc around next BPdc) across to last hdc, hdc in last hdc: {11-14}{16-19-21} V-Sts.

Rows 4 thru {11-15}{17-21-25}: Repeat Rows 2 and 3, {4-6}{7-9-11} times: {7-8}{9-10-10} V-Sts.

Work even until Armhole measures same as Back, ending by working a **wrong** side row.

Finish off.

RIGHT FRONT NECK AND ARMHOLE SHAPING
Row 1: With **right** side of Front facing, skip {5-5}{5-7-7} sts from Left Neck and join yarn with slip st in next hdc; ch 2, work FPdc around next BPdc, (work V-St in next hdc, work FPdc around next BPdc) {12-15}{17-20-22} times, hdc in next hdc, leave remaining {6-6}{8-8-10} sts unworked: {12-15}{17-20-22} V-Sts.

Row 2: Ch 2, turn; work BPdc around next FPdc, (work V-St in next V-St, work BPdc around next FPdc) across to last hdc, hdc in last hdc.

Row 3 (Decrease row): Ch 2, turn; (work FPdc around next BPdc, work V-St in next V-St) across to last 2 BPdc, decrease, hdc in last hdc: {11-14}{16-19-21} V-Sts.

Rows 4 thru {11-15}{17-21-25}: Repeat Rows 2 and 3, {4-6-7-9-11} times: {7-8}{9-10-10} V-Sts.

Work even until Armhole measures same as Back, ending by working a **wrong** side row.

Finish off.

RIBBING AND SKIRT
Work same as Back.

SLEEVE (Make 2)
Ch {41-41}{47-51-55}, place marker in third ch from hook for Ruffle placement.

Row 1: Dc in back ridge of fourth ch from hook and each ch across: {39-39}{45-49-53} sts.

Row 2 (Right side): Ch 2, turn; work FPdc around next dc, (work V-St in next dc, work FPdc around next dc) across to last st, hdc in last st: {18-18}{21-23-25} V-Sts.

Note: Mark Row 2 as **right** side.

Row 3: Ch 2, turn; work BPdc around next FPdc, (work V-St in next V-St, work BPdc around next FPdc) across to last hdc, hdc in last hdc.

Row 4: Ch 2, turn; work FPdc around next BPdc, (work V-St in next V-St, work FPdc around next BPdc) across to last hdc, hdc in last hdc.

Row 5: Repeat Row 3.

SLEEVE CAP
Row 1: Slip st across to {3rd-3rd}{4th-4th-5th} V-St, ch 2, work FPdc around next BPdc, (work V-St in next V-St, work FPdc around next BPdc) across to last {3-3}{4-4-5} V-Sts, hdc in next dc, leave remaining sts unworked: {12-12}{13-15-15} V-Sts.

Row 2: Ch 2, turn; work BPdc around next FPdc, (work V-St in next V-St, work BPdc around next FPdc) across to last hdc, hdc in last hdc.

Row 3 (Decrease row): Ch 2, turn; decrease, work V-St in next V-St, (work FPdc around next BPdc, work V-St in next V-St) across to last 2 BPdc, decrease, hdc in last hdc: {10-10}{11-13-13} V-Sts.

Sizes Small and Medium Only
Rows 4-8: Work even.

Row 9: Repeat Row 3: 8 V-Sts.

Rows 10-15: Repeat Rows 4-9: 6 V-Sts.

Rows 16-18: Work even.

Row 19: Repeat Row 3: 4 V-Sts.

Rows 20-23: Repeat Rows 16-19: 2 V-Sts.

Row 24: Work even; finish off.

Size Large, X-Large, and 2X-Large Only
Rows 4-8: Work even.

Row 9: Repeat Row 3: {9-11-11} V-Sts.

Rows 10-12: Work even.

Rows 13-24: Repeat Rows 9-12, 3 times; then repeat Rows 9 and 10, {0-1-1} time(s) **more (see Zeros, page 94)**: 3 V-Sts.

Finish off.

SLEEVE RUFFLE

Row 1: With **right** side facing and working in free loops of beginning ch, join yarn with slip st in marked ch; ch 2, work FPdc around next dc, (work V-St in next ch, work FPdc around next dc) across to last ch, hdc in last ch: {18-18}{21-23-25} V-Sts.

Row 2: Ch 2, turn; work BPdc around next FPdc, (work V-St in next V-St, work BPdc around next FPdc) across to last hdc, hdc in last hdc.

Row 3: Ch 2, turn; work FPdc around next BPdc, ★ (2 dc, ch 1, dc) in next V-St, work FPdc around next BPdc; repeat from ★ across to last hdc, hdc in last hdc.

Row 4: Ch 2, turn; work BPdc around next FPdc, ★ (2 dc, ch 1, dc) in next ch-1 sp, work BPdc around next FPdc; repeat from ★ across to last hdc, hdc in last hdc.

Row 5: Ch 2, turn; work FPdc around next BPdc, ★ (2 dc, ch 1, 2 dc) in next ch-1 sp, work FPdc around next BPdc; repeat from ★ across to last hdc, hdc in last hdc.

Row 6: Ch 2, turn; work BPdc around next FPdc, ★ (2 dc, ch 1, 2 dc) in next ch-1 sp, work BPdc around next FPdc; repeat from ★ across to last hdc, hdc in last hdc.

Row 7: Ch 2, turn; work FPdc around next BPdc, ★ 6 dc in next ch-1 sp, work FPdc around next BPdc; repeat from ★ across to last hdc, hdc in last hdc; finish off.

FINISHING

With **right** sides together, sew shoulder seams, then set in sleeves, easing if necessary in order to fit. Sew underarm and side seam in one continuous seam.

Neck Edging: With **right** side facing and working in end of rows, join yarn with sc in first row of Right Neck opening **(see Joining with Sc, page 94)**; 6 dc in next row, (sc in next row, 6 dc in next row) across to Back, skip next V-St, (sc in next BPdc, 6 dc in next V-St) across to Left Neck opening; working in end of rows, sc in next row, (6 dc in next row, sc in next row) across to last row, slip st in last row; finish off.

TIE

Leaving a long end, chain a 16" (40.5 cm) length, finish off leaving a long end.

Using photo, page 37, as a guide, lace Tie through center of four 6-dc groups on each side of Front Neck Edging.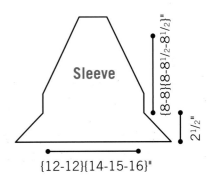

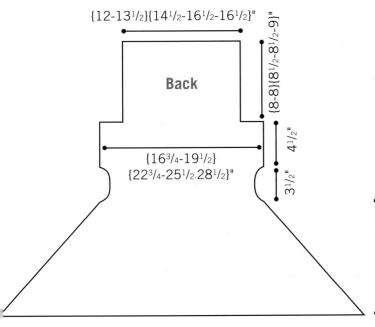

QUINTESSENTIAL

My collection couldn't be called "ultimate" unless it included the little black dress. Now you can make yourself this crocheted version that is perfect for any occasion!

Size	Finished Chest Measurement
Small	27" (68.5 cm)
Medium	30" (76 cm)
Large	35" (89 cm)
X-Large	39" (99 cm)
2X-Large	44" (112 cm)

Size Note: Instructions are written with sizes Small and Medium in the first set of braces { } and sizes Large, X-Large, and 2X-Large in the second set of braces. Instructions will be easier to read if you circle all the numbers pertaining to your size. If only one number is given, it applies to all sizes.

MATERIALS
Medium Weight Yarn 4
[1.75 ounces, 93 yards
(50 grams, 84 meters) per skein]:
   {21-22}{25-27-30} skeins
Crochet hooks, sizes F (3.75 mm) **and**
   K (6.5 mm) **or** sizes needed for gauge
Yarn needle
1" (2.5 cm) wide Non-roll elastic - cut to
   waist measurement plus 1" (2.5 cm)
¾" (19 mm) wide Velvet ribbon -
   2 yards (2 meters)
Sewing needle and matching thread
Convertible-style plunge bra in your size

Photo model made using Nashua Handknits Creative Focus Cotton #0031 Black.

Dress is worked in three pieces, then assembled and sewn to the bra. Leave the straps on the bra as you will sew the Neckline to them. The Skirt and Bodice use different size hooks, so be sure to check your gauge for each.

GAUGES
SKIRT AND NECKLINE
With larger size hook, in pattern,
12 hdc and 9 rows = 4" (10 cm)
BODICE
With smaller size hook, in pattern,
20 sts and 12 rows = 4" (10 cm)

Skirt Gauge Swatch: 4" (10 cm) square
With larger size hook, ch 13.
Row 1: Hdc in second ch from hook and in each ch across: 12 hdc.
Rows 2-9: Ch 1, turn; hdc in Back Loop Only of each hdc across (*Fig. 2, page 95*).
Finish off.

Bodice Gauge Swatch: 4" (10 cm) square
With smaller size hook, ch 22.
Row 1: Dc in fourth ch from hook and in each ch across: 20 sts.
Rows 2-12: Ch 2 (**counts as first hdc**), (work FPdc around next st, work BPdc around next st) across to last st, hdc in last st.
Finish off.

Instructions continued on page 44.

QUINTESSENTIAL

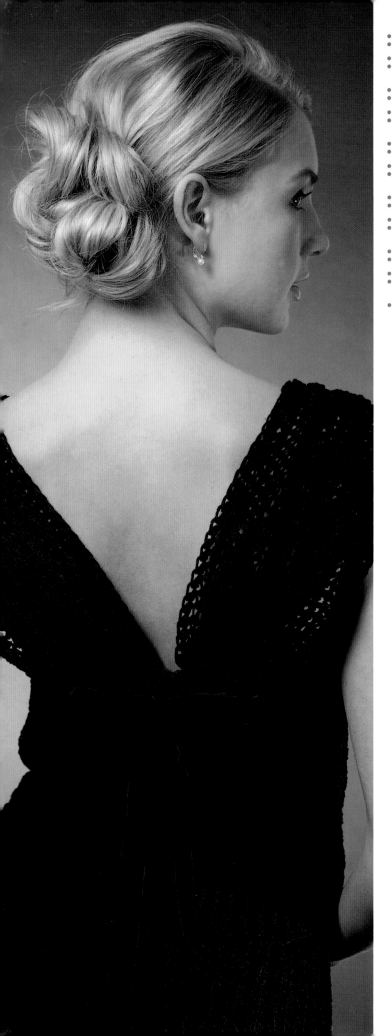

STITCH GUIDE

BACK POST DOUBLE CROCHET
(abbreviated BPdc)

YO, insert hook from **back** to **front** around post of st indicated *(Fig. 4, page 95)*, YO and pull up a loop (3 loops on hook), (YO and draw through 2 loops on hook) twice.

FRONT POST DOUBLE CROCHET
(abbreviated FPdc)

YO, insert hook from **front** to **back** around post of st indicated *(Fig. 4, page 95)*, YO and pull up a loop (3 loops on hook), (YO and draw through 2 loops on hook) twice.

SKIRT

Each row is worked across length of Skirt.

With larger size hook, ch 87.

Row 1 (Wrong side)**:** Hdc in back ridge of second ch from hook and each ch across *(Fig. 1, page 95)*: 86 hdc.

Note: Loop a short piece of yarn around the **back** of any stitch on Row 1 to mark **right** side.

Rows 2 thru {100-108}{118-128-140}: Ch 1, turn; hdc in Back Loop Only of each hdc across *(Fig. 2, page 95)*.

Finish off, leaving a 40" (101.5 cm) length for sewing.

NECKLINE

With larger size hook and leaving a long end for sewing, ch 139.

Row 1 (Wrong side)**:** Hdc in back ridge of second ch from hook and each ch across: 138 hdc.

Note: Mark the **back** of any stitch on Row 1 as **right** side.

Rows 2 thru {16-16}{20-20-24}: Ch 1, turn; hdc in Back Loop Only of each hdc across.

Finish off, leaving a long end for sewing.

BODICE

With smaller size hook, ch {136-152} {176-196-222}.

Row 1 (Wrong side)**:** Dc in back ridge of fourth ch from hook and each ch across: {134-150} {174-194-220} sts.

Note: Mark the **back** of any stitch on Row 1 as **right** side.

Rows 2-25: Ch 2 **(counts as first hdc, now and throughout)**, turn; (work FPdc around next st, work BPdc around next st) across to last st, hdc in last st.

LEFT SHAPING
Sizes Small, Medium, and 2X-Large Only
Row 1: Ch 2, turn; work FPdc around next BPdc, (work BPdc around next FPdc, work FPdc around next BPdc) {10-13}{27} times, hdc in next FPdc, leave remaining {111-121}{163} sts unworked: {23-29}{57} sts.

Row 2: Ch 2, turn; work BPdc around next FPdc, (work FPdc around next BPdc, work BPdc around next FPdc) across to last hdc, hdc in last hdc.

Row 3: Ch 2, turn; work FPdc around next BPdc, (work BPdc around next FPdc, work FPdc around next BPdc) across to last hdc, hdc in last hdc.

Rows 4 and 5: Repeat Rows 2 and 3.

Finish off.

Sizes Large and X-Large Only
Row 1: Ch 2, turn; (work FPdc around next BPdc, work BPdc around next FPdc) {18-22} times, hdc in next BPdc, leave remaining {136-148} sts unworked: {38-46} sts.

Rows 2-5: Ch 2, turn; (work FPdc around next BPdc, work BPdc around next FPdc) across to last hdc, hdc in last hdc.

Finish off.

RIGHT SHAPING
Sizes Small, Medium, and 2X-Large Only
Row 1: With **right** side facing and using smaller size hook, skip next {88-92}{106} sts and join yarn with slip st in next BPdc; ch 2, work BPdc around next FPdc, (work FPdc around next BPdc, work BPdc around next FPdc) across to last hdc, hdc in last hdc: {23-29}{57} sts.

Row 2: Ch 2, turn; work FPdc around next BPdc, (work BPdc around next FPdc, work FPdc around next BPdc) across to last hdc, hdc in last hdc.

Row 3: Ch 2 turn; work BPdc around next FPdc, (work FPdc around next BPdc, work BPdc around next FPdc) across to last hdc, hdc in last hdc.

Rows 4 and 5: Repeat Rows 2 and 3.

Finish off.

Sizes Large and X-Large Only
Row 1: With **right** side facing and using smaller size hook, skip next {98-102} sts and join yarn with slip st in next FPdc; ch 2, (work FPdc around next BPdc, work BPdc around next FPdc) across to last hdc, hdc in last hdc: {38-46} sts.

Instructions continued on page 46.

My best friend Laurie (aka Crazy Aunt Purl) truly has the best fashion sense of anyone I've ever met in real life. Her guidance and advice has been priceless for me as a designer. She tells me often how a criss-cross top like this one is flattering for nearly every woman, so I knew I had to include one in this collection - and name it after her!

◼◼◼◻ **INTERMEDIATE**

Size	Finished Chest Measurement
Small	32" (81.5 cm)
Medium	36" (91.5 cm)
Large	40" (101.5 cm)
X-Large	44" (112 cm)
2X-Large	48" (122 cm)

Size Note: Instructions are written with sizes Small and Medium in the first set of braces { } and sizes Large, X-Large, and 2X-Large in the second set of braces. Instructions will be easier to read if you circle all the numbers pertaining to your size. If only one number is given, it applies to all sizes.

MATERIALS

Light Weight Yarn 🧶③
[1.76 ounces, 120 yards
(50 grams, 110 meters) per hank]:
 {12-13}{15-17-19} hanks
Crochet hook, size F (3.75 mm) **or** size needed
 for gauge
Tapestry needle

Photo model made using Stitch Diva Studios Studio Silk Shrinking Violet.

Each piece of Body is worked across the length of the sweater from Front to center Back, beginning at the Tie. It is very important that your gauge be perfect. So, when you are able to get the stitch gauge you are right on track, but if your row gauge is off you may need to consider using a shorter stitch like a treble crochet or a taller stitch like a triple treble crochet.

GAUGE: In pattern, 20 sts and 6 rows = 4" (10 cm)

Gauge Swatch: 4" (10 cm) square
Ch 24.
Row 1: Dtr in sixth ch from hook **(5 skipped chs count as first dtr)** and in each ch across: 20 dtr.
Row 2: Ch 4 **(counts as first tr, now and throughout)**, turn; work FPdtr around each of next 18 sts, tr in last st.
Row 3: Ch 4, turn; work BPdtr around each FPdtr across, tr in last tr.
Rows 4-6: Repeat Rows 2 and 3 once, then repeat Row 2 once **more**.
Finish off.

Instructions continued on page 50.

LAURIE

STITCH GUIDE

TREBLE CROCHET *(abbreviated tr)*
YO twice, insert hook in st indicated, YO and pull up a loop (4 loops on hook), (YO and draw through 2 loops on hook) 3 times.

DOUBLE TREBLE CROCHET *(abbreviated dtr)*
YO 3 times, insert hook in st indicated, YO and pull up a loop (5 loops on hook), (YO and draw through 2 loops on hook) 4 times.

BACK POST DOUBLE TREBLE CROCHET
(abbreviated BPdtr)
YO 3 times, insert hook from **back** to **front** around post of st indicated *(Fig. 4, page 95)*, YO and pull up a loop (5 loops on hook), (YO and draw through 2 loops on hook) 4 times.

FRONT POST DOUBLE TREBLE CROCHET
(abbreviated FPdtr)
YO 3 times, insert hook from **front** to **back** around post of st indicated *(Fig. 4, page 95)*, YO and pull up a loop (5 loops on hook), (YO and draw through 2 loops on hook) 4 times.

BP DECREASE (uses next 2 FPdtr)
★ YO 3 times, insert hook from **back** to **front** aroundpost of **next** FPtr *(Fig. 4, page 95)*, YO and pull up a loop, (YO and draw through 2 loops on hook) 3 times; repeat from ★ once **more**, YO and draw through all 3 loops on hook **(counts as one BPdtr).**

FP DECREASE (uses next 2 BPdtr)
★ YO 3 times, insert hook from **front** to **back** around post of **next** BPdtr *(Fig. 4, page 95)*, YO and pull up a loop, (YO and draw through 2 loops on hook) 3 times; repeat from ★ once **more**, YO and draw through all 3 loops on hook **(counts as one FPdtr).**

RIGHT FRONT
TIE
Ch 8.

Row 1: Dtr in sixth ch from hook **(5 skipped chs count as first dtr, now and throughout)** and in last 2 chs: 4 dtr.

Row 2: Ch 4 **(counts as first tr, now and throughout)**, turn; work FPdtr around each of next 2 dtr, tr in last dtr.

Row 3: Ch 4, turn; work BPdtr around each of next 2 FPdtr, tr in last tr.

Row 4: Ch 4, turn; work FPdtr around each of next 2 BPdtr, tr in last tr.

Repeat Rows 3 and 4 until Tie measures approximately {40-43}{47-52-56}"/{101.5-109} {119.5-132-142} cm from beginning ch, ending by working Row 4; do **not** finish off.

BODY
Row 1 (Wrong side)**:** Ch 25, turn; dtr in sixth ch from hook and in each ch across, work BPdtr around each of next 3 sts, tr in last tr: 25 sts.

Note: Loop a short piece of yarn around the **back** of any stitch on Row 1 to mark **right** side.

Row 2: Ch 4, turn; work 2 FPdtr around each of next {5-4}{4-3-3} sts, work FPdtr around each dtr across to last tr, tr in last tr: {30-29}{29-28-28} sts.

Row 3: Ch 4, turn; work BPdtr around each FPdtr across to last {6-5}{5-5-4} sts, work 2 BPdtr around each of next {5-4}{4-4-3} FPdtr, tr in last tr: {35-33}{33-32-31} sts.

Row 4: Ch 4, turn; work 2 FPdtr around each of next {5-4}{4-4-3} BPdtr, work FPdtr around each BPdtr across to last tr, tr in last tr: {40-37}{37-36-34} sts.

Row 5 (Increase row): Ch 4, turn; work BPdtr around each FPdtr across to last {6-6}{5-5-4} sts, work 2 BPdtr around each of next {5-5}{4-4-3} FPdtr, tr in last tr: {45-42}{41-40-37} sts.

Row 6 (Increase row): Ch 4, turn; work 2 FPdtr around each of next {5-5}{4-4-3} BPdtr, work FPdtr around each BPdtr across to last tr, tr in last tr: {50-47}{45-44-40} sts.

Rows 7 thru {11-18}{16-23-11}: Repeat Rows 5 and 6, {2-6}{5-8-2} times; then repeat Row 5, {1-0}{0-1-1} time(s) **more** *(see Zeros, page 94)*: {75-107}{85-112-55} sts.

Sizes Small and 2X-Large Only
Row 12 (Increase row): Ch 4, turn; work 2 FPdtr around each of next {6}{4} BPdtr, work FPdtr around each BPdtr across to last tr, tr in last tr: {81}{59} sts.

Row 13 (Increase row): Ch 4, turn; work BPdtr around each FPdtr across to last {7}{5} sts, work 2 BPdtr around each of next {6}{4} FPdtr, tr in last tr: {87}{63} sts.

Rows 14 thru {16}{26}: Repeat Rows 12 and 13, {1}{6} time(s); then repeat Row 12 once **more**: {105}{115} sts.

Size Large Only
Row 17 (Increase row): Ch 4, turn; work BPdtr around each FPdtr across to last 6 sts, work 2 BPdtr around each of next 5 FPdtr, tr in last tr: 90 sts.

Row 18 (Increase row): Ch 4, turn; work 2 FPdtr around each of next 5 BPdtr, work FPdtr around each BPdtr across to last tr, tr in last tr: 95 sts.

Rows 19-21: Repeat Rows 17 and 18 once, then repeat Row 17 once **more**: 110 sts.

All Sizes
Work even until Body measures approximately {13-15}{17-19-21}"/{33-38}{43-48.5-53.5} cm, ending by working a **right** side row; do **not** finish off.

ARMHOLE
Row 1: Ch 4, turn; work BPdtr around each of next {65-68}{68-69-71} FPdtr, tr in next FPdtr, leave remaining {38-37}{40-41-42} sts unworked: {67-70}{70-71-73} sts.

Row 2: Ch 4, turn; work FPdtr around each BPdtr across to last tr, tr in last tr.

Row 3: Ch 4, turn; work BPdtr around each FPdtr across to last tr, tr in last tr.

Rows 4 and 5: Repeat Rows 2 and 3; do **not** finish off.

Instructions continued on page 52.

BACK

Row 1: Ch {42-41}{44-45-46}, turn; dtr in sixth ch from hook and in each ch across, work FPdtr around each BPdtr across to last tr, tr in last tr: {105-107}{110-112-115} sts.

Row 2: Ch 4, turn; work BPdtr around each st across to last st, tr in last st.

Work even until Back measures approximately {6¼-7¼}{8¼-9¼-10¼}"/{16-18.5}{21-23.5-26} cm from Armhole, ending by working a **right** side row; finish off.

LEFT FRONT
TIE

Work same as Right Front Tie until piece measures approximately {63-66}{70-75-79}"/{160-167.5}{178-190.5-200.5} cm from beginning ch, ending by working Row 3, do **not** finish off.

BODY

Row 1 (Right side)**:** Ch 25, turn; dtr in sixth ch from hook and in each ch across, work FPdtr around each of next 3 sts, tr in last tr: 25 sts.

Note: Mark Row 1 as **right** side.

Row 2: Ch 4, turn; work 2 BPdtr around each of next {5-4}{4-3-3} sts, work BPdtr around each dtr across to last tr, tr in last tr: {30-29}{29-28-28} sts.

Row 3: Ch 4, turn; work FPdtr around each BPdtr across to last {6-5}{5-5-4} sts, work 2 FPdtr around each of next {5-4}{4-4-3} BPdtr, tr in last tr: {35-33}{33-32-31} sts.

Row 4: Ch 4, turn; work 2 BPdtr around each of next {5-4}{4-4-3} FPdtr, work BPdtr around each FPdtr across to last tr, tr in last tr: {40-37}{37-36-34} sts.

Row 5 (Increase row): Ch 4, turn; work FPdtr around each BPdtr across to last {6-6}{5-5-4} sts, work 2 FPdtr around each of next {5-5}{4-4-3} BPdtr, tr in last tr: {45-42}{41-40-37} sts.

Row 6 (Increase row): Ch 4, turn; work 2 BPdtr around each of next {5-5}{4-4-3} FPdtr, work BPdtr around each FPdtr across to last tr, tr in last tr: {50-47}{45-44-40} sts.

Rows 7 thru {11-18}{16-23-11}: Repeat Rows 5 and 6, {2-6}{5-8-2} times; then repeat Row 5, {1-0} {0-1-1} time(s) **more**: {75-107}{85-112-55} sts.

Sizes Small and 2X-Large Only
Row 12 (Increase row): Ch 4, turn; work 2 BPdtr around each of next {6}{4} FPdtr, work BPdtr around each FPdtr across to last tr, tr in last tr: {81}{59} sts.

Row 13 (Increase row): Ch 4, turn; work FPdtr around each BPdtr across to last {7}{5} sts, work 2 FPdtr around each of next {6}{4} BPdtr, tr in last tr: {87}{63} sts.

Rows 14 thru {16}{26}: Repeat Rows 12 and 13, {1}{6} time(s); then repeat Row 12 once **more**: {105}{115} sts.

Size Large Only
Row 17 (Increase row): Ch 4, turn; work FPdtr around each BPdtr across to last 6 sts, work 2 FPdtr around each of next 5 BPdtr, tr in last tr: 90 sts.

Row 18 (Increase row): Ch 4, turn; work 2 BPdtr around each of next 5 FPdtr, work BPdtr around each FPdtr across to last tr, tr in last tr: 95 sts.

Rows 19-21: Repeat Rows 17 and 18 once, then repeat Row 17 once **more**: 110 sts.

All Sizes
Work even until Body measures approximately {13-15}{17-19-21}"/{33-38}{43-48.5-53.5} cm, ending by working a **wrong** side row; do **not** finish off.

ARMHOLE
Row 1: Ch 4, turn; work FPdtr around each of next {65-68}{68-69-71} BPdtr, tr in next BPdtr, leave remaining {38-37}{40-41-42} sts unworked: {67-70}{70-71-73} sts.

Row 2: Ch 4, turn; work BPdtr around each FPdtr across to last tr, tr in last tr.

Row 3: Ch 4, turn; work FPdtr around each BPdtr across to last tr, tr in last tr.

Rows 4 and 5: Repeat Rows 2 and 3; do **not** finish off.

BACK
Row 1: Ch {42-41}{44-45-46}, turn; dtr in sixth ch from hook and in each ch across, work BPdtr around each FPdtr across to last tr, tr in last tr: {105-107}{110-112-115} sts.

Row 2: Ch 4, turn; work FPdtr around each st across to last st, tr in last st.

Work even until Back measures approximately {6¼-7¼}{8¼-9¼-10¼}"/{16-18.5}{21-23.5-26} cm from Armhole, ending by working a **right** side row; finish off.

Instructions continued on page 54.

SLEEVE (Make 2)

Ch 51.

Row 1 (Wrong side): Dtr in sixth ch from hook and in each ch across: 47 dtr.

Note: Mark the **back** of any stitch on Row 1 as **right** side.

Row 2 (Increase row): Ch 4, turn; work 2 FPdtr around next st, work FPdtr around each st across to last 2 sts, work 2 FPdtr around next st, tr in last st: 49 sts.

Row 3 (Increase row): Ch 4, turn; work 2 BPdtr around next FPdtr, work BPdtr around each FPdtr across to last 2 sts, work 2 BPdtr around next FPdtr, tr in last tr: 51 sts.

Rows 4 thru {11-14}{15-10-8}: Repeat Rows 2 and 3, {4-5}{6-3-2} times; then repeat Row 2, {0-1}{0-1-1} time(s) **more**: {67-73}{75-65-61} sts.

Sizes Large and 2X-Large Only

Row {11-9} (Increase row): Ch 4, turn; work 2 BPdtr around each of next 2 FPdtr, work BPdtr around each FPdtr across to last 3 sts, work 2 BPdtr around each of next 2 FPdtr, tr in last tr: {69-65} sts.

Row {12-10} (Increase row): Ch 4, turn; work 2 FPdtr around each of next 2 BPdtr, work FPdtr around each BPdtr across to last 3 sts, work 2 FPdtr around each of next 2 BPdtr, tr in last tr: {73-69} sts.

Rows {13-11} thru 14: Repeat Rows {11-9} and {12-10}, {1-2} time(s): {81-85} sts.

All Sizes

Work even until Sleeve measures approximately 10$\frac{1}{2}$" (26.5 cm) from beginning ch, ending by working a **wrong** side row; do **not** finish off.

SLEEVE CAP

Row 1 (Decrease row): Ch 4, turn; work FP decrease 4 times, work FPdtr around each BPdtr across to last 9 sts, work FP decrease 4 times, tr in last tr: {59-65}{67-73-77} sts.

Row 2 (Decrease row): Ch 4, turn; work BP decrease 4 times, work BPdtr around each FPdtr across to last 9 sts, work BP decrease 4 times, tr in last tr: {51-57}{59-65-69} sts.

Sizes Small, Medium, Large, and X-Large Only

Rows 3 thru {6-6}{4-4}: Repeat Rows 1 and 2, {2-2}{1-1} time(s): {19-25}{43-49} sts.

Row {7-7}{5-5}: Ch 4, turn; work FP decrease 3 times, work FPdtr around each BPdtr across to last 7 sts, work FP decrease 3 times, tr in last tr: {13-19}{37-43} sts.

Size Small Only

Finish off.

Size Medium Only

Row 8: Ch 4, turn; work BP decrease 3 times, work BPdtr around each FPdtr across to last 7 sts, work BP decrease 3 times, tr in last tr; finish off: 13 sts.

Size Large Only

Row 6 (Decrease row): Ch 4, turn; work BP decrease 3 times, work BPdtr around each FPdtr across to last 7 sts, work BP decrease 3 times, tr in last tr: 31 sts.

Rows 7-9: Repeat Rows 5 and 6 once, then repeat Row 5 once **more**: 13 sts.

Finish off.

Size X-Large Only

Row 6 (Decrease row): Ch 4, turn; work BP decrease 3 times, work BPdtr around each FPdtr across to last 7 sts, work BP decrease 3 times, tr in last tr: 37 sts.

Rows 7-10: Repeat Rows 5 and 6 twice: 13 sts.

Finish off.

Size 2X-Large Only

Row 3: Ch 4, turn; work FP decrease 4 times, work FPdtr around each BPdtr across to last 9 sts, work FP decrease 4 times, tr in last tr: 61 sts.

Row 4 (Decrease row): Ch 4, turn; work BP decrease 3 times, work BPdtr around each FPdtr across to last 7 sts, work BP decrease 3 times, tr in last tr: 55 sts.

Row 5 (Decrease row): Ch 4, turn; work FP decrease 3 times, work FPdtr around each BPdtr across to last 7 sts, work FP decrease 3 times, tr in last tr: 49 sts.

Rows 6-11: Repeat Rows 4 and 5, 3 times: 13 sts.

Finish off.

ASSEMBLY

With **right** sides together, sew Back seam.

With **right** sides together, sew each shoulder seam.

With **right** sides together, set in each Sleeve and sew underarm seam. 🐘

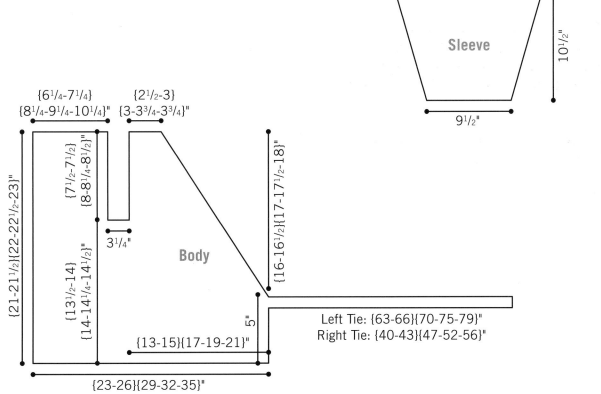

ANGEL OF MUSIC

Inspired by vintage Hollywood glamour, this flouncy little opera jacket has hidden pockets and a faux hood.

■■■□ INTERMEDIATE

Size	Finished Chest Measurement	
Small	39"	(99 cm)
Medium	42"	(106.5 cm)
Large	46"	(117 cm)
X-Large	50"	(127 cm)
2X-Large	54"	(137 cm)

Size Note: Instructions are written with sizes Small and Medium in the first set of braces { } and sizes Large, X-Large, and 2X-Large in the second set of braces. Instructions will be easier to read if you circle all the numbers pertaining to your size. If only one number is given, it applies to all sizes.

MATERIALS
Medium Weight Yarn 🔵④
[1.75 ounces, 97 yards
(50 grams, 88 meters) per skein]:
　{24-25}{27-29-32} skeins
Crochet hook, size H (5 mm) **or** size needed
　for gauge
Yarn needle

Photo model made using Nashua Handknits Julia NHJ.3158 Purple Basil.

GAUGE: In pattern,
　20 sts and 10 rows = 4" (10 cm)

Gauge Swatch: 4" (10 cm) square
Ch 22.
Row 1: Dc in back ridge of fourth ch from hook and each ch across *(Fig. 1, page 95)*: 20 sts.
Row 2: Ch 2 **(counts as first hdc, now and throughout)**, turn; (dc in next dc, work FPdc around next dc) across to last st, hdc in last st.
Row 3: Ch 2, turn; (dc in next FPdc, work FPdc around next dc) across to last hdc, hdc in last hdc.
Row 4: Ch 2, turn; (dc in next FPdc, work FPdc around next dc) across to last hdc, hdc in last hdc.
Rows 5-10: Repeat Rows 3 and 4, 3 times.
Finish off.

Instructions continued on page 58.

STITCH GUIDE

FRONT POST DOUBLE CROCHET
(abbreviated FPdc)

YO, insert hook from **front** to **back** around post of st indicated *(Fig. 4, page 95)*, YO and pull up a loop (3 loops on hook), (YO and draw through 2 loops on hook) twice.

PICOT

Ch 1, sc in top of sc just made *(Fig. 5, page 95)*.

EXTENDED SC *(abbreviated exsc)*

Insert hook in st indicated, YO and pull up a loop, YO and draw through one loop on hook, YO and draw through both loops on hook.

BACK

Ch {99-107}{117-127-137}.

Row 1: Dc in back ridge of fourth ch from hook and each ch across *(Fig. 1, page 95)*: {97-105}{115-125-135} sts.

Row 2 (Right side)**:** Ch 2 **(counts as first hdc, now and throughout)**, turn; work FPdc around next dc, (dc in next dc, work FPdc around next dc) across to last st, hdc in last st.

Note: Loop a short piece of yarn around any stitch to mark Row 2 as **right** side.

Row 3: Ch 2, turn; dc in next FPdc, (work FPdc around next dc, dc in next FPdc) across to last hdc, hdc in last hdc.

Row 4: Ch 2, turn; work FPdc around next dc, (dc in next FPdc, work FPdc around next dc) across to last hdc, hdc in last hdc.

Rows 5-36: Repeat Rows 3 and 4, 16 times.

Finish off.

ARMHOLE SHAPING

Sizes Small, Medium, Large, and 2X-Large Only

Row 1: With **wrong** side facing, skip first {12-14}{16-22} sts and join yarn with slip st in next dc; ch 2, dc in next FPdc, (work FPdc around next dc, dc in next FPdc) across to last {13-15}{17-23} sts, hdc in next dc, leave remaining {12-14}{16-22} sts unworked: {73-77}{83-91} sts.

Row 2: Ch 2, turn; work FPdc around next dc, (dc in next FPdc, work FPdc around next dc) across to last hdc, hdc in last hdc.

Row 3: Ch 2, turn; dc in next FPdc, (work FPdc around next dc, dc in next FPdc) across to last hdc, hdc in last hdc.

Rows 4-24: Repeat Rows 2 and 3, 10 times; then repeat Row 2 once **more**.

Finish off.

Size X-Large Only

Row 1: With **wrong** side facing, skip first 19 sts and join yarn with slip st in next FPdc; ch 2, work FPdc around next dc, (dc in next FPdc, work FPdc around next dc) across to last 20 sts, hdc in next FPdc, leave remaining 19 sts unworked: 87 sts.

Row 2: Ch 2, turn; dc in next FPdc, (work FPdc around next dc, dc in next FPdc) across to last hdc, hdc in last hdc.

Row 3: Ch 2, turn; work FPdc around next dc, (dc in next FPdc, work FPdc around next dc) across to last hdc, hdc in last hdc.

Rows 4-24: Repeat Rows 2 and 3, 10 times; then repeat Row 2 once **more**.

Finish off.

RIGHT FRONT

Ch {51-55}{59-65-69}.

Rows 1-4: Work same as Back: {49-53}{57-63-67} sts.

SIDE POCKET OPENING
Row 5: Ch 2, turn; dc in next FPdc, (work FPdc around next dc, dc in next FPdc) {9-10}{11-13-14} times, hdc in next dc, leave remaining sts unworked: {21-23}{25-29-31} sts.

Row 6: Ch 2, turn; work FPdc around next dc, (dc in next FPdc, work FPdc around next dc) across to last hdc, hdc in last hdc.

Row 7: Ch 2, turn; dc in next FPdc, (work FPdc around next dc, dc in next FPdc) across to last hdc, hdc in last hdc.

Rows 8-16: Repeat Rows 6 and 7, 4 times; then repeat Row 6 once **more**.

Finish off.

FRONT EDGE
Row 5: With **wrong** side facing, join yarn with slip st in first unworked FPdc on Row 4; ch 2, (work FPdc around next dc, dc in next FPdc) across to last hdc, hdc in last hdc: {28-30}{32-34-36} sts.

Rows 6-16: Ch 2, turn; (work FPdc around next dc, dc in next FPdc) across to last hdc, hdc in last hdc.

Finish off.

Instructions continued on page 60.

JOINING

Row 17 (Joining row): With **wrong** side facing, join yarn with slip st in first hdc on Row 16 of Side Pocket Opening; ch 2, dc in next FPdc, (work FPdc around next dc, dc in next FPdc) across to last hdc of Side Pocket Opening, work FPdc around last hdc; working in sts on Row 16 of Front Edge, dc in first hdc, (work FPdc around next dc, dc in next FPdc) across to last hdc, hdc in last hdc: {49-53}{57-63-67} sts.

Row 18: Ch 2, turn; work FPdc around next dc, (dc in next FPdc, work FPdc around next dc) across to last hdc, hdc in last hdc.

Row 19: Ch 2, turn; dc in next FPdc, (work FPdc around next dc, dc in next FPdc) across to last hdc, hdc in last hdc.

Rows 20-36: Repeat Rows 18 and 19, 8 times; then repeat Row 18 once **more**.

Finish off.

ARMHOLE SHAPING

Sizes Small, Medium, Large, and 2X-Large Only

Row 1: With **wrong** side facing, skip first {12-14}{16-22} sts and join yarn with slip st in next dc; ch 2, dc in next FPdc, (work FPdc around next dc, dc in next FPdc) across to last hdc, hdc in last hdc: {37-39}{41-45} sts.

Row 2: Ch 2, turn; work FPdc around next dc, (dc in next FPdc, work FPdc around next dc) across to last hdc, hdc in last hdc.

Row 3: Ch 2, turn; dc in next FPdc, (work FPdc around next dc, dc in next FPdc) across to last hdc, hdc in last hdc.

Rows 4-10: Repeat Rows 2 and 3, 3 times; then repeat Row 2 once **more**; do **not** finish off.

Size X-Large Only

Row 1: With **wrong** side facing, skip first 19 sts and join yarn with slip st in next FPdc; ch 2, (work FPdc around next dc, dc in next FPdc) across to last hdc, hdc in last hdc: 44 sts.

Rows 2-10: Ch 2, turn; (work FPdc around next dc, dc in next FPdc) across to last hdc, hdc in last hdc; do **not** finish off.

NECK SHAPING

Sizes Small, Medium, Large, and 2X-Large Only

Row 1: Ch 2, turn; dc in next FPdc, (work FPdc around next dc, dc in next FPdc) across to last 7 sts, hdc in next dc, leave remaining 6 sts unworked: {31-33}{35-39} sts.

Row 2: Turn; slip st in first 7 sts, ch 2, work FPdc around next dc, (dc in next FPdc, work FPdc around next dc) across to last hdc, hdc in last hdc: {25-27}{29-33} sts.

Rows 3 and 4: Repeat Rows 1 and 2: {13-15}{17-21} sts.

Row 5: Ch 2, turn; dc in next FPdc, (work FPdc around next dc, dc in next FPdc) across to last hdc, hdc in last hdc.

Row 6: Ch 2, turn; work FPdc around next dc, (dc in next FPdc, work FPdc around next dc) across to last hdc, hdc in last hdc.

Rows 7-14: Repeat Rows 5 and 6, 4 times.

Finish off.

Size X-Large Only
Row 1: Ch 2, turn; (work FPdc around next dc, dc in next FPdc) across to last 7 sts, hdc in next dc, leave remaining 6 sts unworked: 38 sts.

Row 2: Turn; slip st in first 7 sts, ch 2, (work FPdc around next dc, dc in next FPdc) across to last hdc, hdc in last hdc: 32 sts.

Rows 3 and 4: Repeat Rows 1 and 2: 20 sts.

Rows 5-14: Ch 2, turn; (work FPdc around next dc, dc in next FPdc) across to last hdc, hdc in last hdc.

Finish off.

LEFT FRONT
Ch {51-55}{59-65-69}.

Rows 1-4: Work same as Back: {49-53}{57-63-67} sts.

FRONT EDGE
Row 5: Ch 2, turn; (dc in next FPdc, work FPdc around next dc) {13-14}{15-16-17} times, hdc in next FPdc, leave remaining {21-23}{25-29-31} sts unworked: {28-30}{32-34-36} sts.

Rows 6-16: Ch 2, turn; (dc in next FPdc, work FPdc around next dc) across to last hdc, hdc in last hdc.

Finish off.

SIDE POCKET OPENING
Row 5: With **wrong** side facing, join yarn with slip st in first unworked dc on Row 4; ch 2, dc in next FPdc, (work FPdc in next dc, dc in next FPdc) across to last hdc, hdc in last hdc: {21-23}{25-29-31} sts.

Row 6: Ch 2, turn; work FPdc around next dc, (dc in next FPdc, work FPdc around next dc) across to last hdc, hdc in last hdc.

Row 7: Ch 2, turn; dc in next FPdc, (work FPdc around next dc, dc in next FPdc) across to last hdc, hdc in last hdc.

Rows 8-16: Repeat Rows 6 and 7, 4 times; then repeat Row 6 once **more**.

Finish off.

JOINING
Row 17: With **wrong** side facing, join yarn with slip st in first hdc on Row 16 of Front Edge; ch 2, (dc in next FPdc, work FPdc around next dc) across to last hdc of Front Edge, dc in last hdc; working in sts on Row 16 of Side Pocket Opening, work FPdc around first hdc, dc in next FPdc, (work FPdc around next dc, dc in next FPdc) across to last hdc, hdc in last hdc: {49-53}{57-63-67} sts.

Rows 18-36: Work same as Right Front; at end of Row 36, do **not** finish off.

ARMHOLE SHAPING
Sizes Small, Medium, Large, and 2X-Large Only
Row 1: Ch 2, turn; dc in next FPdc, (work FPdc around next dc, dc in next FPdc) {17-18}{19-21} times, hdc in next dc, leave remaining {12-14}{16-22} sts unworked: {37-39}{41-45} sts.

Instructions continued on page 62.

Row 2: Ch 2, turn; work FPdc around next dc, (dc in next FPdc, work FPdc around next dc) across to last hdc, hdc in last hdc.

Row 3: Ch 2, turn; dc in next FPdc, (work FPdc around next dc, dc in next FPdc) across to last hdc, hdc in last hdc.

Rows 4-10: Repeat Rows 2 and 3, 3 times; then repeat Row 2 once **more**; do **not** finish off.

Size X-Large Only
Row 1: Ch 2, turn; (dc in next FPdc, work FPdc around next dc) 21 times, hdc in next dc, leave remaining 19 sts unworked: 44 sts.

Rows 2-10: Ch 2, turn; (dc in next FPdc, work FPdc around next dc) across to last hdc, hdc in last hdc; do **not** finish off.

NECK SHAPING
Sizes Small, Medium, Large, and 2X-Large Only
Row 1: Turn; slip st in first 7 sts, ch 2, dc in next FPdc, (work FPdc around next dc, dc in next FPdc) across to last hdc, hdc in last hdc: {31-33}{35-39} sts.

Row 2: Ch 2, turn; work FPdc around next dc, (dc in next FPdc, work FPdc around next dc) across to last 7 sts, hdc in next FPdc, leave remaining 6 sts unworked: {25-27}{29-33} sts.

Rows 3 and 4: Repeat Rows 1 and 2: {13-15}{17-21} sts.

Row 5: Ch 2, turn; dc in next FPdc, (work FPdc around next dc, dc in next FPdc) across to last hdc, hdc in last hdc.

Row 6: Ch 2, turn; work FPdc around next dc, (dc in next FPdc, work FPdc around next dc) across to last hdc, hdc in last hdc.

Rows 7-14: Repeat Rows 5 and 6, 4 times.

Finish off.

Size X-Large Only
Row 1: Turn; slip st in first 7 sts, ch 2, (dc in next FPdc, work FPdc around next dc) across to last hdc, hdc in last hdc: 38 sts.

Row 2: Ch 2, turn; (dc in next FPdc, work FPdc around next dc) across to last 7 sts, hdc in next FPdc, leave remaining 6 sts unworked: 32 sts.

Rows 3 and 4: Repeat Rows 1 and 2: 20 sts.

Rows 5-14: Ch 2, turn; (dc in next FPdc, work FPdc around next dc) across to last hdc, hdc in last hdc.

Finish off.

POCKET (Make 2)
Ch 21.

Row 1: Sc in back ridge of second ch from hook and each ch across: 20 sc.

Rows 2-10: Ch 1, turn; sc in each sc across.

Finish off.

Placing Pocket on **wrong** side of either Front, sew end of rows to end of rows on Side Pocket Opening; continue to sew remaining 3 edges of Pocket to Front.

POCKET EDGING

Row 1: With **right** side of Front facing and working in end of rows across Front Edge, join yarn with sc in first row; work 20 sc evenly spaced across: 21 sc.

Row 2: Ch 1, turn; sc in each sc across.

Row 3: Ch 1, turn; sc in first sc, (work Picot, skip next sc, sc in next sc) across; finish off.

Sew ends of Pocket Edging to Front.

Repeat for second Pocket.

SLEEVE (Make 2)

Ch 62, place marker in third ch from hook for st placement.

Row 1: Dc in back ridge of fourth ch from hook and each ch across: 60 sts.

Row 2 (Right side): Ch 2, turn; (dc in next dc, work FPdc around next dc) across to last st, hdc in last st.

Note: Mark Row 2 as **right** side.

Row 3 (Increase row): Ch 2, turn; dc in same st and in next st, work FPdc around next dc, (dc in next FPdc, work FPdc around next dc) across to last hdc, (dc, hdc) in last hdc: 62 sts.

Row 4 (Increase row): Ch 2, turn; dc in same st, (work FPdc around next dc, dc in next st) across to last hdc, (dc, hdc) in last hdc: 64 sts.

Rows 5-13: Repeat Rows 3 and 4, 4 times; then repeat Row 3 once **more**: 82 sts.

Row 14: Ch 2, turn; work FPdc around next dc, (dc in next FPdc, work FPdc around next dc) across to last 2 sts, dc in next dc, hdc in last hdc.

Rows 15 thru {20-21}{22-23-25}: Ch 2, turn; (work FPdc around next dc, dc in next FPdc) across to last hdc, hdc in last hdc.

Finish off.

CUFF

Row 1: With **right** side facing and working in free loops of beginning ch *(Fig. 3, page 95)*, join yarn with sc in marked ch *(see Joining With Sc, page 94)*; sc in next ch and in each ch across: 60 sc.

Rows 2-10: Ch 1, turn; sc in each sc across.

Finish off.

TIE (Make 2)

Ch 9.

Row 1: Dc in back ridge of fourth ch from hook and each ch across: 7 sts.

Row 2 (Right side): Ch 2, turn; work FPdc around next dc, (dc in next dc, work FPdc around next dc) twice, hdc in last dc.

Note: Mark Row 2 as **right** side.

Instructions continued on page 64.

Row 3: Ch 2, turn; dc in next FPdc, (work FPdc around next dc, dc in next FPdc) twice, hdc in last hdc.

Row 4: Ch 2, turn; work FPdc around next dc, (dc in next FPdc, work FPdc around next dc) twice, hdc in last hdc.

Rows 5-56: Repeat Rows 3 and 4, 26 times.

Finish off.

BACK TAB
Ch 9.

Row 1 (Right side): Sc in back ridge of second ch from hook and each ch across: 8 sc.

Note: Mark Row 1 as **right** side.

Rows 2-16: Ch 1, turn; sc in each sc across.

Edging: Ch 1, turn; sc in first sc, work Picot, (skip next sc, sc in next sc, work Picot) 3 times, skip last sc; † working in end of rows, sc in first row, work Picot, (skip next row, sc in next row, work Picot) 7 times, skip last row †; working in free loops of beginning ch, sc in first ch, work Picot, (skip next ch, sc in next ch, work Picot) 3 times, skip last ch; repeat from † to † once; join with slip st to first sc, finish off.

FINISHING
With **right** sides together, sew shoulder seams.

Set in Sleeves *(Fig. A)*.

Fig. A

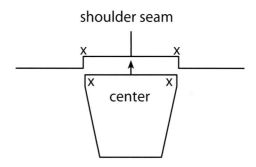

Sew underarm and side in one continuous seam.

Turn up Cuffs and tack in place if desired.

Using photo as a guide, page 59, sew Back Tab to center Back at waist.

COLLAR
Row 1: With **wrong** side facing, join yarn with sc in first unworked st on Back neck; sc in next st and in each st across: {47-47}{49-47-49} sc.

Row 2: Ch 1, turn; work exsc in each sc across; working in end of rows on Left Front, work 2 exsc in first row: {49-49}{51-49-51} exsc.

Row 3: Ch 1, turn; work exsc in each exsc across; working in end of rows on Right Front, work 2 exsc in first row: {51-51}{53-51-53} exsc.

Rows 4-21: Ch 1, turn; work exsc in each exsc across; work 2 exsc in end of next row: {53-53}{55-53-55} exsc.

Rows 22-29: Ch 1, turn; work exsc in each exsc across; working in sts on Front, work exsc in next 6 sts: {101-101}{103-101-103} exsc.

Rows 30-33: Ch 1, turn; work exsc in each exsc across.

Finish off.

JACKET EDGING

Rnd 1: With **right** side facing, join yarn with sc in any st on bottom edge; sc evenly around entire piece working an even number of sc; join with slip st to first sc.

Rnd 2: Ch 1, sc in same st, work Picot, skip next sc, (sc in next sc, work Picot, skip next sc) around; join with slip st to first sc, finish off.

Sew each Tie to **wrong** side just before neckline decreasing.

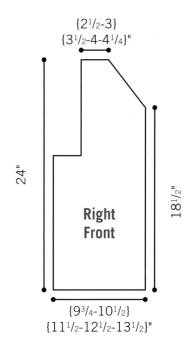

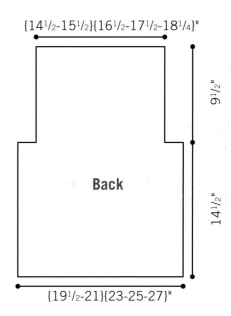

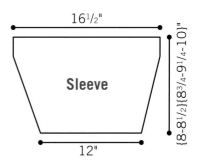

SAUGATUCK SUMMER

One of my favorite teenage memories is of walking the docks of my hometown in Michigan called Saugatuck with my buddies in the summertime. It was lined with yacht after yacht of the Chicago elite on vacation. Even more fabulous were the clothes they wore, and this boatneck top is inspired by that look. Hidden cables around the waist create a flattering fit without interrupting the lines of the ribbing.

■■■□ INTERMEDIATE

Size	Finished Chest Measurement
Small	28" (71 cm)
Medium	30½" (77.5 cm)
Large	34½" (87.5 cm)
X-Large	39" (99 cm)
2X-Large	43" (109 cm)

Size Note: Instructions are written with sizes Small and Medium in the first set of braces { } and sizes Large, X-Large, and 2X-Large in the second set of braces. Instructions will be easier to read if you circle all the numbers pertaining to your size. If only one number is given, it applies to all sizes.

MATERIALS

Light Weight Yarn
[1.75 ounces, 125 yards
(50 grams, 114 meters) per ball]:
   {10-10}{12-13-15} balls
Crochet hook, size H (5 mm) **or** size needed
   for gauge
Yarn needle
Round cord elastic - 30" (76 cm)
Safety pin

Photo model made using Plymouth Yarn® Baby Alpaca DK #1580.

GAUGE: In pattern,
      19 sts and 14 rows/rnds = 4" (10 cm)

Gauge Swatch: 4" (10 cm) square
Ch 21.
Row 1: Dc in fourth ch from hook and in each ch across: 19 sts.
Row 2: Ch 3 **(counts as first dc, now and throughout)**, turn; work FPdc around next st, (work BPdc around next st, work FPdc around next st) across to last st, dc in last st.
Row 3: Ch 3, turn; work BPdc around next FPdc, (work FPdc around next BPdc, work BPdc around next FPdc) across to last dc, dc in last dc.
Rows 4-14: Repeat Rows 2 and 3, 5 times; then repeat Row 2 once **more**.
Finish off.

Instructions continued on page 68.

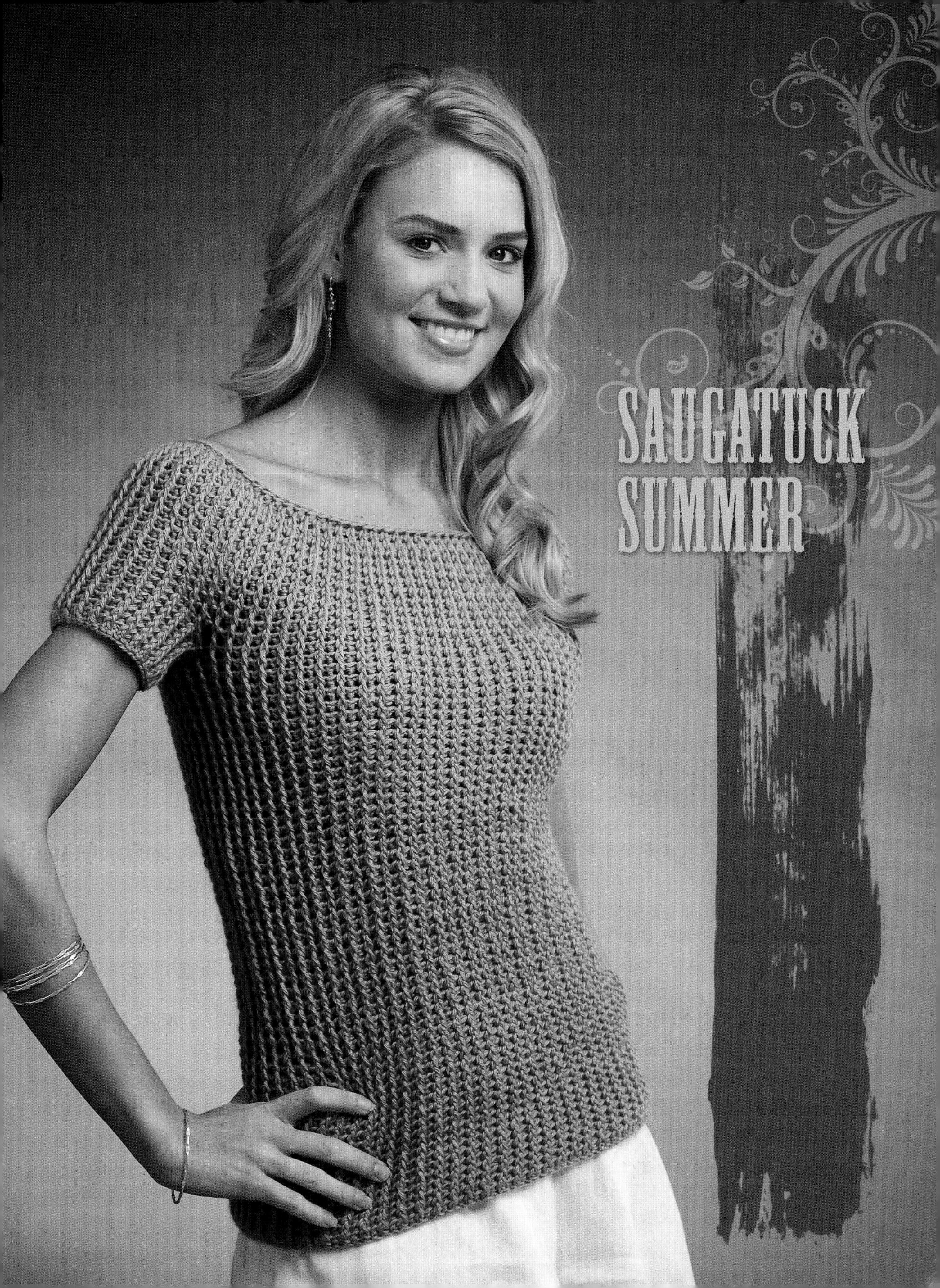

SAUGATUCK SUMMER

The pattern is worked in the round creating a tube for the Body. Sleeves are worked independently in the round, then all three pieces are joined and worked in the round to form the Yoke.

BODY

Ch {132-144}{164-184-204}; being careful **not** to twist ch, join with slip st to form a ring.

Rnd 1 (Right side): Ch 3 **(counts as first dc, now and throughout)**, dc in back ridge of next ch **(Fig. 1, page 95)** and each ch around; do **not** join, place marker to mark beginning of rnd **(see Markers, page 94)**: {132-144}{164-184-204} dc.

Rnd 2: (Work BPdc around next dc, work FPdc around next dc) around.

Rnd 3: (Work BPdc around next BPdc, work FPdc around next FPdc) around.

Repeat Rnd 3 until Body measures approximately 6" (15 cm) from beginning ch.

WAIST SHAPING

Rnd 1: (Work Cable, work FPdc around next FPdc) around.

Rnds 2 and 3: (Work BPdc around next BPdc, work FPdc around next FPdc) around.

Rnd 4: (Work Cable, work FPdc around next FPdc) around.

Rnds 5-16: Repeat Rnds 2-4, 4 times.

Repeat Rnd 2 until piece measures approximately 16" (40.5 cm) from beginning ch; do **not** finish off, remove marker and place loop from hook onto safety pin to prevent piece from unraveling while working Sleeves.

STITCH GUIDE

BACK POST DOUBLE CROCHET
(abbreviated BPdc)

YO, insert hook from **back** to **front** around post of st indicated **(Fig. 4, page 95)**, YO and pull up a loop (3 loops on hook), (YO and draw through 2 loops on hook) twice.

FRONT POST DOUBLE CROCHET
(abbreviated FPdc)

YO, insert hook from **front** to **back** around post of st indicated **(Fig. 4, page 95)**, YO and pull up a loop (3 loops on hook), (YO and draw through 2 loops on hook) twice.

CABLE (uses 3 sts)

Skip next 2 sts, work BPdc around next BPdc, working in **front** of BPdc just made, work FPdc around skipped FPdc, working **behind** FPdc just made, work BPdc around skipped BPdc.

SLEEVE (Make 2)

Ch {40-40}{46-52-58}; being careful **not** to twist ch, join with slip st to form a ring.

Rnd 1 (Right side): Ch 3, dc in back ridge of next ch and each ch around; do **not** join, place marker to mark beginning of rnd: {40-40}{46-52-58} dc.

Work same as Body until Sleeve measures approximately 2" (5 cm) from beginning ch **or** to desired length; join with slip st to next BPdc, finish off leaving a long end for sewing.

YOKE

Rnd 1: Place loop from safety pin onto hook. With **right** side of Body and one Sleeve facing, † work BPdc around joined BPdc on Sleeve, work FPdc around next FPdc, (work BPdc around next BPdc, work FPdc around next FPdc) around to last 6 sts, leave remaining sts on Sleeve unworked †; skip next 6 sts on Body, (work BPdc around next BPdc, work FPdc around next FPdc) {30-33} {38-43-48} times; with **right** side of second Sleeve facing, repeat from † to † once, skip next 6 sts on Body, (work BPdc around next BPdc, work FPdc around next FPdc) around; do **not** join, place marker to mark beginning of rnd: {188-200} {232-264-296} sts.

Rnd 2: (Work BPdc around next BPdc, work FPdc around next FPdc) around.

Repeat Rnd 2 until piece measures approximately 19" (48.5 cm) from beginning ring.

Next Rnd: (Dc in next BPdc, work FPdc around next FPdc) around.

Next Rnd: (Skip next dc, work FPdc around next FPdc) around.

Last Rnd: Work FPdc around each FPdc around; join with slip st to next FPdc, finish off.

FINISHING

Weave elastic through the **wrong** side of the sts on the last rnd and tie ends securely.

Thread needle with end from one Sleeve and sew seam at underarm.

Repeat for second Sleeve.

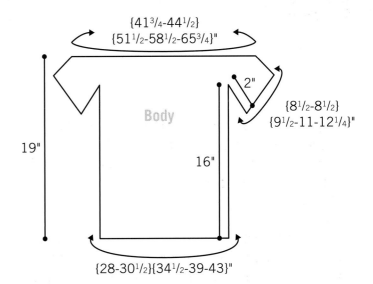

HESPERAS

Crochet goes all the way with this strapless bustier party dress. Surprisingly quick to make, too!

■■■□ INTERMEDIATE

Size	Finished Chest Measurement
Small	32" (81.5 cm)
Medium	36" (91.5 cm)
Large	40" (101.5 cm)
X-Large	44" (112 cm)

Size Note: Instructions are written for size Small with sizes Medium, Large, and X-Large in braces { }. Instructions will be easier to read if you circle all the numbers pertaining to your size. If only one number is given, it applies to all sizes.

MATERIALS

Medium Weight Yarn **④**
[1.75 ounces, 164 yards
(50 grams, 150 meters) per hank]:
   Pink - 4{4-5-5} hanks
Medium Weight Novelty Yarn
[1.75 ounces, 60 yards
(50 grams, 55 meters) per hank]:
   Sequin - 10{11-12-14} hanks
Crochet hooks, sizes F (3.75 mm) **and**
   I (5.5 mm) **or** sizes needed for gauge
Yarn needle
Markers
Strapless bustier in your size
Sewing needle and matching thread
Straight pins
Fabric for underskirt - 10" wide x 48" long
   (25.5 cm x 122 cm)
6" (15 cm) wide Tulle netting for ruffle - 5 yards
   (4.5 meters)

Photo model made using South West Trading Company Yin #823 Movement and Yang #839 Action.

GAUGES
Bodice
In pattern, with smaller size hook and Sequin, 22 sts and 14 rows = 4" (10 cm)
Skirt
In pattern, with larger size hook and Pink, 9 sts and 12 rows = 4" (10 cm)

Bodice Gauge Swatch: 4" (10 cm) square
With smaller size hook and Sequin, ch 24.
Row 1: Dc in fourth ch from hook and in each ch across: 22 sts.
Rows 2-14: Ch 2 (**counts as first hdc**), turn; (work FPdc around next st, work BPdc around next st) across to last st, hdc in last st.
Finish off.

Skirt Gauge Swatch: 4" wide x 4¼" high
(10 cm x 10.75 cm)
With larger size hook and Pink, ch 11.
Row 1: Dc in fourth ch from hook and in each ch across: 9 sts.
Rows 2-14: Work same as Skirt Rows 3-15, page 76.
Finish off.

Instructions continued on page 72.

HESPERAS

STITCH GUIDE

TREBLE CROCHET *(abbreviated tr)*
YO twice, insert hook in st indicated, YO and pull up a loop (4 loops on hook), (YO and draw through 2 loops on hook) 3 times.

BACK POST DOUBLE CROCHET
(abbreviated BPdc)
YO, insert hook from **back** to **front** around post of st indicated *(Fig. 4, page 95)*, YO and pull up a loop (3 loops on hook), (YO and draw through 2 loops on hook) twice.

FRONT POST DOUBLE CROCHET
(abbreviated FPdc)
YO, insert hook from **front** to **back** around post of st indicated *(Fig. 4, page 95)*, YO and pull up a loop (3 loops on hook), (YO and draw through 2 loops on hook) twice.

BACK POST TREBLE CROCHET
(abbreviated BPtr)
YO twice, insert hook from **back** to **front** around post of st indicated *(Fig. 4, page 95)*, YO and pull up a loop (4 loops on hook), (YO and draw through 2 loops on hook) 3 times.

FRONT POST TREBLE CROCHET
(abbreviated FPtr)
YO twice, insert hook from **front** to **back** around post of st indicated *(Fig. 4, page 95)*, YO and pull up a loop (4 loops on hook), (YO and draw through 2 loops on hook) 3 times.

DECREASE
Pull up a loop in next 2 sts, YO and draw through all 3 loops on hook **(counts as one sc)**.

BODICE

With smaller size hook and using Sequin, ch 138{152-174-202}.

Row 1: Sc in back ridge of second ch from hook and each ch across *(Fig. 1, page 95)*: 137{151-173-201} sc.

Row 2 (Right side)**:** Ch 2 **(counts as first hdc, now and throughout)**, turn; work FPdc around next sc, (work BPdc around next sc, work FPdc around next sc) across to last sc, hdc in last sc.

Note: Loop a short piece of yarn around any stitch to mark Row 2 as **right** side.

Row 3: Ch 2, turn; work BPdc around next FPdc, (work FPdc around next BPdc, work BPdc around next FPdc) across to last hdc, hdc in last hdc.

Row 4: Ch 2, turn; work FPdc around next BPdc, (work BPdc around next FPdc, work FPdc around next BPdc) across to last hdc, hdc in last hdc.

Rows 5-20: Repeat Rows 3 and 4, 8 times.

RIGHT SIDE SHAPING
Sizes Small, Large, and X-Large Only
Row 1: Ch 2, turn; (work BPdc around next FPdc, work FPdc around next BPdc) 24{30-37} times, hdc in next FPdc, leave remaining 87{111-125} sts unworked: 50{62-76} sts.

Row 2 (Decrease row)**:** Ch 2, turn; skip next 2 sts, (work BPdc around next FPdc, work FPdc around next BPdc) across to last hdc, hdc in last hdc: 48{60-74} sts.

Row 3 (Decrease row)**:** Ch 2, turn; (work BPdc around next FPdc, work FPdc around next BPdc) across to last 3 sts, skip next 2 sts, hdc in last hdc: 46{58-72} sts.

Rows 4 and 5: Repeat Rows 2 and 3: 42{54-68} sts.

Row 6 (Decrease row)**:** Ch 2, turn; skip next FPdc, work FPdc around next BPdc, (work BPdc around next FPdc, work FPdc around next BPdc) across to last hdc, hdc in last hdc: 41{53-67} sts.

Row 7 (Decrease row): Ch 2, turn; (work BPdc around next FPdc, work FPdc around next BPdc) across to last 2 sts, skip next FPdc, hdc in last hdc: 40{52-66} sts.

Rows 8 and 9: Repeat Rows 6 and 7: 38{50-64} sts.

Finish off.

Size Medium Only
Row 1: Ch 2, turn; work BPdc around next FPdc, (work FPdc around next BPdc, work BPdc around next FPdc) 27 times, hdc in next BPdc, leave remaining 94 sts unworked: 57 sts.

Row 2 (Decrease row): Ch 2, turn; skip next 2 sts, work FPdc around next BPdc, (work BPdc around next FPdc, work FPdc around next BPdc) across to last hdc, hdc in last hdc: 55 sts.

Row 3 (Decrease row): Ch 2, turn; work BPdc around next FPdc, (work FPdc around next BPdc, work BPdc around next FPdc) across to last 3 sts, skip next 2 sts, hdc in last hdc: 53 sts.

Rows 4 and 5: Repeat Rows 2 and 3: 49 sts.

Row 6 (Decrease row): Ch 2, turn; skip next BPdc, (work BPdc around next FPdc, work FPdc around next BPdc) across to last hdc, hdc in last hdc: 48 sts.

Row 7 (Decrease row): Ch 2, turn; work BPdc around next FPdc, (work FPdc around next BPdc, work BPdc around next FPdc) across to last 2 sts, skip next BPdc, hdc in last hdc: 47 sts.

Rows 8 and 9: Repeat Rows 6 and 7: 45 sts.

Finish off.

Instructions continued on page 74.

CENTER SHAPING

Sizes Small, Large, and X-Large Only

Row 1: With **wrong** side facing, skip next 5{11-11} sts from Right Side Shaping and join Sequin with slip st in next FPdc; ch 2, work FPdc around next BPdc, (work BPdc around next FPdc, work FPdc around next BPdc) 12 times, hdc in next FPdc, leave remaining 55{73-87} sts unworked: 27 sts.

Row 2 (Decrease row): Ch 2, turn; skip next 2 sts, work BPdc around next FPdc, (work FPdc around next BPdc, work BPdc around next FPdc) across to last 3 sts, skip next 2 sts, hdc in last hdc: 23 sts.

Row 3 (Decrease row): Ch 2, turn; skip next 2 sts, work FPdc around next BPdc, (work BPdc around next FPdc, work FPdc around next BPdc) across to last 3 sts, skip next 2 sts, hdc in last hdc: 19 sts.

Rows 4 and 5: Repeat Rows 2 and 3: 11 sts.

Row 6 (Decrease row): Ch 2, turn; skip next FPdc, work FPdc around next BPdc, (work BPdc around next FPdc, work FPdc around next BPdc) across to last 2 sts, skip next FPdc, hdc in last hdc: 9 sts.

Row 7: Repeat Row 6: 7 sts.

Row 8: Ch 2, turn; skip next FPdc, work FPdc around next BPdc, work BPdc around next FPdc, work FPdc around next BPdc, skip next FPdc, hdc in last hdc: 5 sts.

Row 9: Ch 2, turn; work BPdc around next FPdc, work FPdc around next BPdc, work BPdc around next FPdc, hdc in last hdc; finish off.

Size Medium Only

Row 1: With **wrong** side facing and using smaller size hook, skip next 5 sts from Right Side Shaping and join Sequin with slip st in next BPdc; ch 2, work BPdc around next FPdc, (work FPdc around next BPdc, work BPdc around next FPdc) 12 times, hdc in next BPdc, leave remaining 62 sts unworked: 27 sts.

Row 2 (Decrease row): Ch 2, turn; skip next 2 sts, work FPdc around next BPdc, (work BPdc around next FPdc, work FPdc around next BPdc) across to last 3 sts, skip next 2 sts, hdc in last hdc: 23 sts.

Row 3 (Decrease row): Ch 2, turn; skip next 2 sts, work BPdc around next FPdc, (work FPdc around next BPdc, work BPdc around next FPdc) across to last 3 sts, skip next 2 sts, hdc in last hdc: 19 sts.

Rows 4 and 5: Repeat Rows 2 and 3: 11 sts.

Row 6 (Decrease row): Ch 2, turn; skip next BPdc, work BPdc around next FPdc, (work FPdc around next BPdc, work BPdc around next FPdc) across to last 2 sts, skip next BPdc, hdc in last hdc: 9 sts.

Row 7: Repeat Row 6: 7 sts.

Row 8: Ch 2, turn; skip next BPdc, work BPdc around next FPdc, work FPdc around next BPdc, work BPdc around next FPdc, skip next BPdc, hdc in last hdc: 5 sts.

Row 9: Ch 2, turn; work FPdc around next BPdc, work BPdc around next FPdc, work FPdc around next BPdc, hdc in last hdc; finish off.

LEFT SIDE SHAPING

Sizes Small, Large, and X-Large Only

Row 1: With **wrong** side facing and using smaller size hook, skip next 5{11-11} sts from Center Shaping and join Sequin with slip st in next FPdc; ch 2, (work FPdc around next BPdc, work BPdc around next FPdc) across to last hdc, hdc in last hdc: 50{62-76} sts.

Row 2 (Decrease row): Ch 2, turn; (work FPdc around next BPdc, work BPdc around next FPdc) across to last 3 sts, skip next 2 sts, hdc in last hdc: 48{60-74} sts.

Row 3 (Decrease row)**:** Ch 2, turn; skip next 2 sts, (work FPdc around next BPdc, work BPdc around next FPdc) across to last hdc, hdc in last hdc: 46{58-72} sts.

Rows 4 and 5: Repeat Rows 2 and 3: 42{54-68} sts.

Row 6 (Decrease row)**:** Ch 2, turn; work FPdc around next BPdc, (work BPdc around next FPdc, work FPdc around next BPdc) across to last 2 sts, skip next FPdc, hdc in last hdc: 41{53-67} sts.

Row 7 (Decrease row)**:** Ch 2, turn; skip next FPdc, (work FPdc around next BPdc, work BPdc around next FPdc) across to last hdc, hdc in last hdc: 40{52-66} sts.

Rows 8 and 9: Repeat Rows 6 and 7: 38{50-64} sts.

Finish off.

Size Medium Only
Row 1: With **wrong** side facing and using smaller size hook, skip next 5 sts from Center Shaping and join Sequin with slip st in next BPdc; ch 2, work BPdc around next FPdc, (work FPdc around next BPdc, work BPdc around next FPdc) across to last hdc, hdc in last hdc: 57 sts.

Row 2 (Decrease row)**:** Ch 2, turn; work FPdc around next BPdc, (work BPdc around next FPdc, work FPdc around next BPdc) across to last 3 sts, skip next 2 sts, hdc in last hdc: 55 sts.

Row 3 (Decrease row)**:** Ch 2, turn; skip next 2 sts, work BPdc around next FPdc, (work FPdc around next BPdc, work BPdc around next FPdc) across to last hdc, hdc in last hdc: 53 sts.

Rows 4 and 5: Repeat Rows 2 and 3: 49 sts.

Row 6 (Decrease row)**:** Ch 2, turn; (work FPdc around next BPdc, work BPdc around next FPdc) across to last 2 sts, skip next BPdc, hdc in last hdc: 48 sts.

Row 7 (Decrease row)**:** Ch 2, turn; skip next BPdc, work BPdc around next FPdc, (work FPdc around next BPdc, work BPdc around next FPdc) across to last hdc, hdc in last hdc: 47 sts.

Rows 8 and 9: Repeat Rows 6 and 7: 45 sts.

Finish off.

LEFT CUP
Row 1: With **right** side of Bodice facing, using smaller size hook, and working in end of rows on Left Side and Center Shaping, join Sequin with sc in end of Row 9 on Left Side Shaping *(see Joining With Sc, page 94)*; work 43{43-51-51} sc evenly spaced across through Row 9 of Center Shaping: 44{44-52-52} sc.

Row 2: Ch 1, turn; sc in first 20{20-24-24} sc, decrease twice, sc in next sc, place marker around st just made for decrease placement, sc in each sc across: 42{42-50-50} sc.

Rows 3 thru 17{17-21-21}: Ch 1, turn; sc in each sc across to marked sc, remove marker, decrease twice, sc in next sc, move marker to sc just made, sc in each st across: 12 sc.

Finish off, leaving a long end for sewing.

Matching sts on last row, fold Cup in half with **right** side together. Thread yarn needle with long end and whipstitch across *(Fig. 6a, page 96)*.

Instructions continued on page 76.

RIGHT CUP

Row 1: With **right** side of Bodice facing, using smaller size hook, and working in end of rows on Center and Right Side Shaping, join Sequin with sc in end of Row 9 on Center Shaping; work 43{43-51-51} sc evenly spaced across through Row 9 of Right Side Shaping: 44{44-52-52} sc.

Rows 3 thru 17{17-21-21}: Complete same as Left Cup.

TOP EDGING

Row 1: With **right** side facing, using smaller size hook, and working across top edge of Bodice, join Pink with sc in first st; sc evenly across.

Row 2: Ch 1, turn; sc in each sc across.

Row 3: Ch 1, turn; sc in Back Loop Only of each sc across **(Fig. 2, page 95)**.

Row 4: Ch 1, turn; sc in both loops of each sc across; finish off.

SKIRT

Row 1: With **right** side of Bodice facing, using smaller size hook, and working in free loops of beginning ch **(Fig. 3, page 95)**, join Sequin with sc in first ch; sc in each ch across, cut Sequin: 137{151-173-201} sc.

Change to larger size hook and Pink.

Row 2: Ch 3 **(counts as first dc)**, turn; 2 dc in next sc, (dc in next sc, 2 dc in next sc) across to last sc, 1{2-1-1} dc in last sc: 205{227-259-301} dc.

Row 3: Ch 5 **(counts as first tr plus ch 1)**, turn; ★ skip next dc, work FPtr around next dc, ch 1; repeat from ★ across to last 2 dc, skip next dc, tr in last dc: 103{114-130-151} sts and 102{113-129-150} ch-1 sps.

Row 4: Ch 1, turn; sc in first tr, ch 1, sc in next ch-1 sp, (ch 2, sc in next ch-1 sp) across to last tr, ch 1, sc in last tr.

Row 5: Ch 4 **(counts as first tr, now and throughout)**, turn; work BPtr around next FPtr one row **below**, (ch 1, work BPtr around next st one row **below**) across.

Row 6: Ch 1, turn; sc in first BPtr, ch 1, sc in next ch-1 sp, (ch 2, sc in next ch-1 sp) across to last tr, ch 1, sc in last tr.

Row 7: Ch 4, turn; work BPtr around next BPtr one row **below**, (ch 1, work BPtr around next BPtr one row **below**) across.

Repeat Rows 6 and 7 for pattern until Skirt measures approximately 21" (53.5 cm), ending by working Row 6.

Finish off, leaving a long end for sewing.

FINISHING

Fold last 2 rows of Top Edging to **wrong** side over edge of bustier and pin in place. With sewing needle and thread, stitch last row of Edging in place. Sew across bottom edge of each cup, then sew across bottom edge and back opening, easing in if necessary.

Thread yarn needle with long end on Skirt. With **right** side together, sew seam leaving last 5" (12.5 cm) free.

Place 4 markers evenly spaced on last round of Skirt. Thread yarn needle with a 20" (51 cm) length of Pink. With **wrong** side facing and beginning at marked st, secure end at bottom edge, then weave strand through back of rows up to top of Skirt. Pull strand to raise edge of Skirt to measure 3" (7.5 cm) shorter than rest of Skirt; then secure end. Repeat at each remaining marker.

Sew short ends of fabric together to form a tube. Turn $1/4$" (7 mm) of each long edge under to form a hem and a top edge. Sew netting to hem. Sew top edge of fabric to **wrong** side on Row 3 of Skirt, leaving an 8" (20.5 cm) gap at the back opening.

With smaller size hook and Pink, make a chain 50" (127 cm) in length; finish off.

Use chain to lace up the top opening of the Skirt and bottom edge of Bodice, using end of rows.

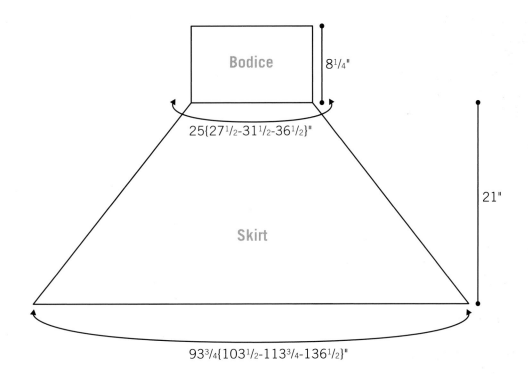

VASHTI

My friend Vashti always wears the most amazing crocheted items whenever I see her, which is usually at some crochet-centric event. They always drape and move and are very eye catching. She inspired me to design this skirt that has maximum movement and style!

◖◗◗◗◻ **INTERMEDIATE**

Size	Finished Waist Measurement
Small	25" (63.5 cm)
Medium	29" (73.5 cm)
Large	33" (84 cm)
X-Large	37" (94 cm)
2X-Large	41" (104 cm)

Finished Length: 38" (96.5 cm)

Size Note: Instructions are written with sizes Small and Medium in the first set of braces { } and sizes Large, X-Large, and 2X-Large in the second set of braces. Instructions will be easier to read if you circle all the numbers pertaining to your size. If only one number is given, it applies to all sizes.

MATERIALS

Light Weight Yarn 🔵 **3** LIGHT
[1.75 ounces, 137 yards
(50 grams, 125 meters) per hank]:
   {11-12}{14-15-17} hanks
Crochet hook, size E (3.5 mm) **or** size needed
   for gauge
Yarn needle
1" (2.5 cm) wide Elastic - cut to Empire waist
   measurement plus 1" (2.5 cm)
Sewing needle and matching thread
2" (5 cm) Cabone ring

Photo model made using Fibra Natura® Flax #12 Tarragon.

GAUGE: In pattern, 17 sts = 4" (10 cm);
                  2 rows = 1" (2.5 cm)

Gauge Swatch: 4$\frac{1}{2}$" x 1" (11.5 cm x 2.5 cm)
Ch 21.
Work same as Strip, page 80.
Finish off.

Instructions continued on page 80.

VASHTI

STITCH GUIDE

BACK POST DOUBLE CROCHET
(abbreviated BPdc)

YO, insert hook from **back** to **front** around post of st indicated *(Fig. 4, page 95)*, YO and pull up a loop (3 loops on hook), (YO and draw through 2 loops on hook) twice.

FRONT POST DOUBLE CROCHET
(abbreviated FPdc)

YO, insert hook from **front** to **back** around post of st indicated *(Fig. 4, page 95)*, YO and pull up a loop (3 loops on hook), (YO and draw through 2 loops on hook) twice.

The Skirt is made of strips that are joined together with chains. Elastic is sewn into the waist, then the decorative belt is worked separately and sewn to the waist.

STRIP [Make {19-21}{23-25-27}]

Each Strip measures 1" x 39" (2.5 cm x 99 cm).

Ch 169, place marker in third ch from hook for st placement.

Row 1: Dc in back ridge of fourth ch from hook *(Fig. 1, page 95)* and each ch across: 167 sts.

Row 2 (Right side): Ch 2 **(counts as first hdc, now and throughout)**, turn; (work FPdc around next st, work BPdc around next st) across to last st, hdc in last st; finish off.

Note: Loop a short piece of yarn around first hdc on Row 2 to mark **right** side **and** bottom edge.

ASSEMBLY

With **right** sides of two Strips facing, bottom edges at same end, and using diagram as a guide, join yarn with sc in first hdc of First Strip *(see Joining With Sc, page 94)*; ch 15, working in free loops of beginning ch *(Fig. 2, page 95)*, sc in marked ch on **next Strip**, [ch 15, skip next 3 sts on **First Strip**, sc in next st, ch 15, skip next 3 chs on **next Strip**, sc in next ch] 7 times, [ch 12, skip next 3 sts on **First Strip**, sc in next st, ch 12, skip next 3 chs on **next Strip**, sc in next ch] 7 times, [ch 9, skip next 3 sts on **First Strip**, sc in next st, ch 9, skip next 3 chs on **next Strip**, sc in next ch] 7 times, [ch 6, skip next 3 sts on **First Strip**, sc in next st, ch 6, skip next 3 chs on **next Strip**, sc in next ch] 7 times, [ch 3, skip next 3 sts on **First Strip**, sc in next st, ch 3, skip next 3 chs on **next Strip**, sc in next ch] 7 times, [ch 1, skip next 3 sts on **First Strip**, sc in next st, ch 1, skip next 3 chs on **next Strip**, sc in next ch] 6 times, ch 1, skip next st on **First Strip**, sc in last hdc, ch 1, skip next ch on **next Strip**, sc in last ch; finish off.

Repeat until all Strips are joined, then join the first and the last Strips together, creating a tube.

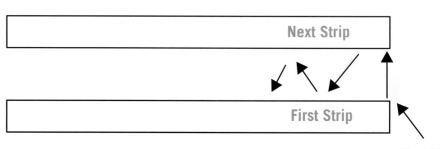

FINISHING

Overlapping ends of elastic ½" (12 mm), sew ends together securely to create waistband. Holding elastic in place on **wrong** side, fold top edge of skirt to cover elastic and whipstitch in place **(Fig. 6a, page 96)**.

BELT

Foundation Rnd: Join yarn with sc around carbone ring; work sc around ring until it's completely covered; join with slip st to first sc, do **not** finish off.

Row 1 (Right side): Ch 2, dc in next 19 sc, hdc in next sc, leave remaining sts unworked: 21 sts.

Note: Mark Row 1 as **right** side.

Row 2: Ch 2, turn; work FPdc around next st, (work BPdc around next st, work FPdc around next st) across to last hdc, hdc in last hdc.

Row 3: Ch 2, turn; work BPdc around next st, (work FPdc around next st, work BPdc around next st) across to last hdc, hdc in last hdc.

Repeat Rows 2 and 3 until Belt measures approximately 50" (127 cm) excluding ring; finish off.

Sew **wrong** side of Row 1 to Skirt waist.

INVESTING

Look sharp from the office to coffee haus! Faux lapels created with diagonally slanted cables make this ladies' vest as easy to wear, as it is to make.

Size	Finished Chest Measurement
Small	30" (76 cm)
Medium	34" (86.5 cm)
Large	38" (96.5 cm)

Size Note: Instructions are written for size Small with sizes Medium and Large in braces { }. Instructions will be easier to read if you circle all the numbers pertaining to your size. If only one number is given, it applies to all sizes.

MATERIALS

Light Weight Yarn (3)
[1.75 ounces, 161 yards,
(50 grams, 147 meters) per skein]:
  6{7-8} skeins
Crochet hook, size G (4 mm) **or** size needed
  for gauge
Yarn needle
Sewing needle and matching thread
¹/₂" (12 mm) Buttons - 12

*Photo model made using Patons®
Astra #02849 Navy.*

GAUGE: In pattern,
  20 sts and 11 rows = 4" (10 cm)

Gauge Swatch: 5"w x 4"h (12.75 cm x 10 cm)
Ch 27.
Row 1: Dc in fourth ch from hook and in each ch across: 25 sts.
Row 2: Ch 2 **(counts as first hdc, now and throughout)**, turn; work FPdc around next st, (work BPdc around next st, work FPdc around next st) across to last st, hdc in last st.
Row 3: Ch 2, turn; work BPdc around next FPdc, (work FPdc around next BPdc, work BPdc around next FPdc) across to last hdc, hdc in last hdc.
Rows 4-11: Repeat Rows 2 and 3, 4 times.
Finish off.

Instructions continued on page 84.

INVESTING

STITCH GUIDE

BACK POST DOUBLE CROCHET
(abbreviated BPdc)
YO, insert hook from **back** to **front** around post of st indicated *(Fig. 4, page 95)*, YO and pull up a loop (3 loops on hook), (YO and draw through 2 loops on hook) twice.

FRONT POST DOUBLE CROCHET
(abbreviated FPdc)
YO, insert hook from **front** to **back** around post of st indicated *(Fig. 4, page 95)*, YO and pull up a loop (3 loops on hook), (YO and draw through 2 loops on hook) twice.

3-ST CABLE (uses 3 sts)
Skip next 2 sts, work FPdc around next BPdc, working **behind** FPdc just made, work BPdc around second skipped st, working in **front** of last 2 sts made, work FPdc around first skipped st.

FP CABLE (uses next 2 BPdc)
Skip next BPdc, work FPdc around next BPdc, working in **front** of st just made, work FPdc around skipped BPdc.

PICOT
Ch 1, sc in top of sc just made *(Fig. 5, page 95)*.

BACK

Ch 77{87-97}.

Row 1: Dc in back ridge of fourth ch from hook *(Fig. 1, page 95)* and each ch across: 75{85-95} sts.

Row 2 (Right side)**:** Ch 2 **(counts as first hdc, now and throughout)**, turn; work FPdc around next dc, (work BPdc around next dc, work FPdc around next dc) across to last st, hdc in last st.

Note: Loop a short piece of yarn around any stitch to mark Row 2 as **right** side.

Row 3: Ch 2, turn; work BPdc around next FPdc, (work FPdc around next BPdc, work BPdc around next FPdc) across to last hdc, hdc in last hdc.

Row 4: Ch 2, turn; work FPdc around next BPdc, (work BPdc around next FPdc, work FPdc around next BPdc) across to last hdc, hdc in last hdc.

Rows 5-11: Repeat Rows 3 and 4, 3 times; then repeat Row 3 once **more**.

Row 12: Ch 2, turn; (work FPdc around next BPdc, work BPdc around next FPdc) 12{15-17} times, ★ work 3-St Cable, work BPdc around next FPdc; repeat from ★ 5 times **more**, work FPdc around next BPdc, (work BPdc around next FPdc, work FPdc around next BPdc) across to last hdc, hdc in last hdc.

Row 13: Ch 2, turn; work BPdc around next FPdc, (work FPdc around next BPdc, work BPdc around next FPdc) across to last hdc, hdc in last hdc.

Rows 14-22: Repeat Rows 12 and 13, 4 times; then repeat Row 12 once **more**.

Rows 23 thru 33{37-41}: Repeat Rows 3 and 4, 5{7-9} times; then repeat Row 3 once **more**.

Finish off.

LEFT FRONT

Ch 39{45-49}.

Row 1: Dc in back ridge of fourth ch from hook and each ch across: 37{43-47} sts.

To mark pattern placement, lay a short piece of scrap yarn before next stitch when indicated and move it up as each row is worked. You will be increasing one stitch on each **right** side row and decreasing one stitch on each **wrong** side row.

Row 2 (Right side)**:** Ch 2, turn; (work FPdc around next dc, work BPdc around next dc) across to last 4 sts, place marker, work 2 FPdc around next dc, work BPdc around next dc, work FPdc around next dc, hdc in last st: 38{44-48} sts.

Note: Mark Row 2 as **right** side.

Row 3: Ch 2, turn; work BPdc around next FPdc, work FPdc around next BPdc, work BPdc around each of next 2 FPdc, work FPdc around next BPdc, (work BPdc around next FPdc, work FPdc around next BPdc) across to last 2 sts, skip next FPdc, hdc in last hdc: 37{43-47} sts.

Row 4: Ch 2, turn; work BPdc around next FPdc, (work FPdc around next BPdc, work BPdc around next FPdc) across to marker, skip next BPdc, work FPdc around next BPdc, working in **front** of st just made, work 2 FPdc around skipped BPdc, work BPdc around next FPdc, work FPdc around next BPdc, hdc in last hdc: 38{44-48} sts.

Row 5: Ch 2, turn; work BPdc around next FPdc, work FPdc around next BPdc, work BPdc around each FPdc across to marker, (work FPdc around next BPdc, work BPdc around next FPdc) across to last 2 sts, skip next BPdc, hdc in last hdc: 37{43-47} sts.

Row 6: Ch 2, turn; (work FPdc around next BPdc, work BPdc around next FPdc) across to marker, work FP Cable, work 2 FPdc around next BPdc, work BPdc around next FPdc, work FPdc around next BPdc, hdc in last hdc: 38{44-48} sts.

Row 7: Ch 2, turn; work BPdc around next FPdc, work FPdc around next BPdc, work BPdc around each FPdc across to marker, work FPdc around next BPdc, (work BPdc around next FPdc, work FPdc around next BPdc) across to last 2 sts, skip next FPdc, hdc in last hdc: 37{43-47} sts.

Row 8: Ch 2, turn; work BPdc around next FPdc, (work FPdc around next BPdc, work BPdc around next FPdc) across to marker, work FP Cable, skip next BPdc, work 2 FPdc around next BPdc, working in **front** of sts just made, work FPdc around skipped BPdc, work BPdc around next FPdc, work FPdc around next BPdc, hdc in last hdc: 38{44-48} sts.

Row 9: Repeat Row 5: 37{43-47} sts.

Row 10: Ch 2, turn; (work FPdc around next BPdc, work BPdc around next FPdc) across to marker, work FP Cable twice, work 2 FPdc around next BPdc, work BPdc around next FPdc, work FPdc around next BPdc, hdc in last hdc: 38{44-48} sts.

Row 11: Repeat Row 7: 37{43-47} sts.

Row 12: Ch 2, turn; work BPdc around next FPdc, (work FPdc around next BPdc, work BPdc around next FPdc) across to marker, work FP Cable across to last 5 sts, skip next BPdc, work 2 FPdc around next BPdc, working in **front** of sts just made, work FPdc around skipped BPdc, work BPdc around next FPdc, work FPdc around next BPdc, hdc in last hdc: 38{44-48} sts.

Row 13: Repeat Row 5: 37{43-47} sts.

Row 14: Ch 2, turn; (work FPdc around next BPdc, work BPdc around next FPdc) across to marker, work FP Cable across to last 4 sts, work 2 FPdc around next BPdc, work BPdc around next FPdc, work FPdc around next BPdc, hdc in last hdc: 38{44-48} sts.

Rows 15 thru 33{37-41}: Repeat Rows 11-14, 4{5-6} times; then repeat Rows 11-13 once **more**; at end of last row, finish off: 37{43-47} sts.

LEFT STRAP
Row 1: With **right** side facing, join yarn with slip st in 6th st before marker; ch 2, work BPdc around next FPdc, (work FPdc around next BPdc, work BPdc around next FPdc) twice, remove marker, work FP Cable across to last 4 sts, work FPdc around next BPdc, work BPdc around next FPdc, work FPdc around next BPdc, hdc in last hdc: 26{28-30} sts.

Instructions continued on page 86.

Row 2: Ch 2, turn; work BPdc around next FPdc, work FPdc around next BPdc, work BPdc around each FPdc across to last 6 sts, (work FPdc around next BPdc, work BPdc around next FPdc) twice, skip next BPdc, hdc in last hdc: 25{27-29} sts.

Row 3: Ch 2, turn; (work FPdc around next BPdc, work BPdc around next FPdc) twice, work FP Cable across to last 4 sts, skip next BPdc, work BPdc around next FPdc, work FPdc around next BPdc, hdc in last hdc: 24{26-28} sts.

Row 4: Ch 2, turn; work BPdc around next FPdc, work FPdc around next BPdc, work BPdc around each FPdc across to last 5 sts, work FPdc around next BPdc, work BPdc around next FPdc, work FPdc around next BPdc, skip next FPdc, hdc in last hdc: 23{25-27} sts.

Row 5: Ch 2, turn; skip next FPdc, work FPdc around next BPdc, work BPdc around next FPdc, work FP Cable across to last 3 sts, work BPdc around next FPdc, work FPdc around next BPdc, hdc in last hdc: 22{24-26} sts.

Row 6: Ch 2, turn; work BPdc around next FPdc, work FPdc around next BPdc, work BPdc around each FPdc across to last 4 sts, skip next FPdc, work FPdc around next BPdc, work BPdc around next FPdc, hdc in last hdc: 21{23-25} sts.

Row 7: Ch 2, turn; work FPdc around next BPdc, work BPdc around next FPdc, work FPdc around next BPdc, work FP Cable across to last 3 sts, work BPdc around next FPdc, work FPdc around next BPdc, hdc in last hdc.

Row 8: Ch 2, turn; work BPdc around next FPdc, work FPdc around next BPdc, work BPdc around each FPdc across to last 4 sts, skip next FPdc, work FPdc around next BPdc, work BPdc around next FPdc, hdc in last hdc: 20{22-24} sts.

Row 9: Ch 2, turn; work FPdc around next BPdc, work BPdc around next FPdc, work FP Cable across to last 3 sts, work BPdc around next FPdc, work FPdc around next BPdc, hdc in last hdc.

Rows 10 thru 17{21-25}: Repeat Rows 6-9, 2{3-4} times: 16 sts.

Row 18{22-26}: Ch 2, turn; work BPdc around next FPdc, work FPdc around next BPdc, work BPdc around each FPdc across to last 3 sts, work FPdc around next BPdc, work BPdc around next FPdc, hdc in last hdc.

Row 19{23-27}: Ch 2, turn; work FPdc around next BPdc, work BPdc around next FPdc, work FP Cable across to last 3 sts, work BPdc around next FPdc, work FPdc around next BPdc, hdc in last hdc.

Repeat last 2 rows for pattern until Strap measures approximately 14½" (37 cm); finish off leaving a long end for sewing.

BUTTON BAND

Row 1: With **right** side facing and working in end of rows, join yarn with slip st in Row 29; ch 3 **(counts as first dc, now and throughout)**, 2 dc in next row and in each row across to last row, dc in last row: 56 dc.

Row 2: Ch 2, turn; (work BPdc around next dc, work FPdc around next dc) across to last dc, hdc in last dc.

Row 3: Ch 2, turn; (work BPdc around next FPdc, work FPdc around next BPdc) across to last hdc, hdc in last hdc, finish off.

RIGHT FRONT
Ch 39{45-49}.

Row 1: Dc in back ridge of fourth ch from hook and each ch across: 37{43-47} sts.

To mark pattern placement, lay a short piece of scrap yarn before next stitch when indicated and move it up as each row is worked.

Row 2 (Right side)**:** Ch 2, turn; work FPdc around next dc, work BPdc around next dc, work 2 FPdc around next dc, place marker around last FPdc made, (work BPdc around next dc, work FPdc around next dc) across to last st, hdc in last st: 38{44-48} sts.

Note: Mark Row 2 as **right** side.

Row 3: Ch 2, turn; skip next FPdc, work FPdc around next BPdc, (work BPdc around next FPdc, work FPdc around next BPdc) across to marker, work BPdc around each of next 2 FPdc, work FPdc around next BPdc, work BPdc around next FPdc, hdc in last hdc: 37{43-47} sts.

Row 4: Ch 2, turn; work FPdc around next BPdc, work BPdc around next FPdc, skip next BPdc, work FPdc around next BPdc, working in **front** of st just made, work 2 FPdc around skipped BPdc, work BPdc around next FPdc, (work FPdc around next BPdc, work BPdc around next FPdc) across to last hdc, hdc in last hdc: 38{44-48} sts.

Row 5: Ch 2, turn; skip next BPdc, (work BPdc around next FPdc, work FPdc around next BPdc) across to marker, work BPdc around each of next 3 FPdc, work FPdc around next BPdc, work BPdc around next FPdc, hdc in last hdc: 37{43-47} sts.

Row 6: Ch 2, turn; work FPdc around next BPdc, work BPdc around next FPdc, work 2 FPdc around next BPdc, work FP Cable, (work BPdc around next FPdc, work FPdc around next BPdc) across to last hdc, hdc in last hdc: 38{44-48} sts.

Row 7: Ch 2, turn; skip next FPdc, work FPdc around next BPdc, (work BPdc around next FPdc, work FPdc around next BPdc) across to marker, work BPdc around each FPdc across to last 3 sts, work FPdc around next BPdc, work BPdc around next FPdc, hdc in last hdc: 37{43-47} sts.

Row 8: Ch 2, turn; work FPdc around next BPdc, work BPdc around next FPdc, skip next BPdc, work FPdc around next BPdc, working in **front** of st just made, work 2 FPdc around skipped BPdc, work FP Cable, work BPdc around next FPdc, (work FPdc around next BPdc, work BPdc around next FPdc) across to last hdc, hdc in last hdc: 38{44-48} sts.

Row 9: Ch 2, turn; skip next BPdc, (work BPdc around next FPdc, work FPdc around next BPdc) across to marker, work BPdc around each FPdc across to last 3 sts, work FPdc around next BPdc, work BPdc around next FPdc, hdc in last hdc: 37{43-47} sts.

Row 10: Ch 2, turn; work FPdc around next BPdc, work BPdc around next FPdc, work 2 FPdc around next BPdc, work FP Cable twice, (work BPdc around next FPdc, work FPdc around next BPdc) across to last hdc, hdc in last hdc: 38{44-48} sts.

Row 11: Repeat Row 7: 37{43-47} sts.

Instructions continued on page 88.

Row 12: Ch 2, turn; work FPdc around next BPdc, work BPdc around next FPdc, skip next BPdc, work FPdc around next BPdc, working in **front** of st just made, work 2 FPdc around skipped BPdc, work FP Cable across to marker, work BPdc around next FPdc, (work FPdc around next BPdc, work BPdc around next FPdc) across to last hdc, hdc in last hdc: 38{44-48} sts.

Row 13: Repeat Row 9: 37{43-47} sts.

Row 14: Ch 2, turn; work FPdc around next BPdc, work BPdc around next FPdc, work 2 FPdc around next BPdc, work FP Cable across to marker, (work BPdc around next FPdc, work FPdc around next BPdc) across to last hdc, hdc in last hdc: 38{44-48} sts.

Rows 15 thru 33{37-41}: Repeat Rows 11-14, 4{5-6} times; then repeat Rows 11-13 once **more**: 37{43-47} sts.

RIGHT STRAP
Row 1: Ch 2, turn; work FPdc around next BPdc, work BPdc around next FPdc, work FPdc around next BPdc, work FP Cable across to marker, work BPdc around next FPdc, (work FPdc around next BPdc, work BPdc around next FPdc) twice, hdc in next BPdc, leave remaining 5 sts unworked: 26{28-30} sts.

Row 2: Ch 2, turn; skip next BPdc, (work BPdc around next FPdc, work FPdc around next BPdc) twice, work BPdc around each FPdc across to last 3 sts, work FPdc around next BPdc, work BPdc around next FPdc, hdc in last hdc: 25{27-29} sts.

Row 3: Ch 2, turn; work FPdc around next BPdc, work BPdc around next FPdc, skip next 2 BPdc, work FPdc around next BPdc, working in **front** of st just made, work FPdc around second skipped BPdc, work FP Cable across to marker, (work BPdc around next FPdc, work FPdc around BPdc) twice, hdc in last dc: 24{26-28} sts.

Row 4: Ch 2, turn; skip next FPdc, work FPdc around next BPdc, work BPdc around next FPdc, work FPdc around next BPdc, work BPdc around each FPdc across to last 3 sts, work FPdc around next BPdc, work BPdc around next FPdc, hdc in last hdc: 23{25-27} sts.

Row 5: Ch 2, turn; work FPdc around next BPdc, work BPdc around next FPdc, work FP Cable across to marker, remove marker, work BPdc around next FPdc, work FPdc around next BPdc, skip next FPdc, hdc in last hdc: 22{24-26} sts.

Row 6: Ch 2, turn; work BPdc around next FPdc, work FPdc around next BPdc, skip next FPdc, work BPdc around each FPdc across to last 3 sts, work FPdc around next BPdc, work BPdc around next FPdc, hdc in last hdc: 21{23-25} sts.

Row 7: Ch 2, turn; work FPdc around next BPdc, work BPdc around next FPdc, work FP Cable across to last 4 sts, work FPdc around next BPdc, work BPdc around next FPdc, work FPdc around next BPdc, hdc in last hdc.

Row 8: Ch 2, turn; work BPdc around next FPdc, work FPdc around next BPdc, skip next FPdc, work BPdc around each FPdc across to last 3 sts, work FPdc around next BPdc, work BPdc around next FPdc, hdc in last hdc: 20{22-24} sts.

Row 9: Ch 2, turn; work FPdc around next BPdc, work BPdc around next FPdc, work FP Cable across to last 3 sts, work BPdc around next FPdc, work FPdc around next BPdc, hdc in last hdc.

Rows 10 thru 17{21-25}: Repeat Rows 6-9, 2{3-4} times: 16 sts.

Row 18{22-26}: Ch 2, turn; work BPdc around next FPdc, work FPdc around next BPdc, work BPdc around each FPdc across to last 3 sts, work FPdc around next BPdc, work BPdc around next FPdc, hdc in last hdc.

Row 19{23-27}: Ch 2, turn; work FPdc around next BPdc, work BPdc around next FPdc, work FP Cable across to last 3 sts, work BPdc around next FPdc, work FPdc around next BPdc, hdc in last hdc.

Repeat last 2 rows for pattern until Strap measures approximately 14¹/₂" (37 cm); finish off.

BUTTONHOLE BAND

Row 1: With **right** side facing and working in end of rows, join yarn with slip st in Row 1, ch 3, 2 dc in each row across to Row 29, dc in Row 29: 56 dc.

Row 2 (Buttonhole row): Ch 2, turn; ★ work BPdc around next dc, work FPdc around next dc, work BPdc around next dc, ch 1, skip next dc; repeat from ★ 11 times **more**, (work BPdc around next dc, work FPdc around next dc) 3 times, hdc in last dc: 12 ch-1 sps.

Row 3: Ch 2, turn; (work BPdc around next FPdc, work FPdc around next BPdc) 3 times, ★ dc in next ch-1 sp, work FPdc around next BPdc, work BPdc around next FPdc, work FPdc around next BPdc; repeat from ★ across to last hdc, hdc in last hdc; finish off.

FINISHING

With **right** sides together, sew side seams.

Thread needle with long end from Left Strap. With **right** sides together, whipstitch ends of Straps together **(Fig. 6a, page 96)**.

Sew buttons to button band opposite buttonholes.

BACK AND STRAP EDGING

Rnd 1: With **right** side of top edge of Back facing, join yarn with sc in any st **(see Joining With Sc, page 94)**; work Picot, (sc, work Picot) evenly spaced around; join with slip st to first sc, finish off.

BODY AND STRAP EDGING

Rnd 1: With **right** side of bottom edge of Back facing, join yarn with sc in free loop of any ch on beginning ch **(Fig. 3, page 95)**; work Picot, (sc, work Picot) evenly spaced around; join with slip st to first sc, finish off. 🐘

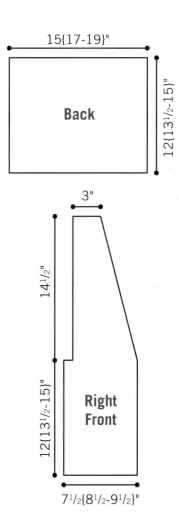

KEYHOLE SCARF

This style of scarf makes it easy to get a custom fit whether you are bundled up for a blizzard or just looking stylish for a holiday party. Makes a great gift too!

⬛⬛⬛⬜ **INTERMEDIATE**

Finished Size: 4" x 36" (10 cm x 91.5 cm)

MATERIALS
Light Weight Yarn 3
[1.76 ounces, 125 yards
(50 grams, 114 meters) per ball]:
  Brown - 2 balls
  Peach - 1 ball
Crochet hook, size H (5 mm) **or** size needed
  for gauge

Photo model made using Plymouth Yarn® Baby Alpaca DK #5046 Peach and #208 Brown.

GAUGE: In pattern, 8 sts and 8 rows = 4" (10 cm)

Gauge Swatch: 4" (10 cm) square
Ch 10.
Row 1: Dc in fourth ch from hook and in each ch across: 8 sts.
Rows 2-8: Ch 3 **(counts as first dc)**, turn; dc in next dc and in each dc across.
Finish off.

STITCH GUIDE

STITCH GUIDE
BACK POST DOUBLE CROCHET
  (abbreviated BPdc)
YO, insert hook from **back** to **front** around post of st indicated *(Fig. 4, page 95)*, YO and pull up a loop (3 loops on hook), (YO and draw through 2 loops on hook) twice.
FRONT POST DOUBLE CROCHET
  (abbreviated FPdc)
YO, insert hook from **front** to **back** around post of st indicated *(Fig. 4, page 95)*, YO and pull up a loop (3 loops on hook), (YO and draw through 2 loops on hook) twice.
ADDING ON DOUBLE CROCHETS
YO, insert hook into base of last dc made *(Fig. A)*, YO and pull up a loop, YO and draw through one loop on hook, (YO and draw through 2 loops on hook) twice. Repeat as many times as instructed.

Fig. A

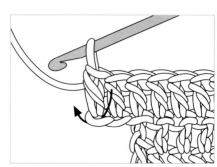

Instructions continued on page 92.

KEYHOLE
SCARF

BODY

With Brown, ch 77.

Rnd 1 (Right side): 4 Dc in fourth ch from hook **(3 skipped chs count as first dc)**, dc in back ridge of next ch and each ch across to last ch **(Fig. 1, page 95)**, 5 dc in last ch; working in free loops of beginning ch **(Fig. 3, page 95)**, dc in each ch across; join with slip st to first dc: 154 dc.

Note: Loop a short piece of yarn around any stitch to mark Row 1 as **right** side.

Rnd 2: Slip st from **back** to **front** around post of same st, ch 3 **(counts as first BPdc)**, work FPdc around next dc, (work BPdc around next dc, work FPdc around next dc) 39 times, YO, insert hook in dc just worked around, YO and pull up a loop, YO and draw through one loop on hook, (YO and draw through 2 loops on hook) twice (first dc added on), add on 18 dc **(Fig. A, page 91)**, YO, insert hook in base of last dc made **and** in next dc on Rnd 1, YO and pull up a loop, (YO and draw through 2 loops on hook) twice, work BPdc around same dc just worked into, work FPdc around next dc, (work BPdc around next dc, work FPdc around next dc) around; join with slip st to first BPdc: 174 sts.

Rnd 3: Slip st from **back** to **front** around post of same st, ch 3 **(counts as first BPdc)**, work 3 FPdc around next FPdc, (work BPdc around next st, work 3 FPdc around next st) around; join with slip st to first BPdc, finish off.

Rnd 4: With **right** side facing, join Peach with a BPdc around any BPdc **(see Joining With BPdc, page 95)**; skip next FPdc, work 3 FPdc around next FPdc, skip next FPdc, ★ work BPdc around next BPdc, skip next FPdc, work 3 FPdc around next FPdc, skip next FPdc; repeat from ★ around; join with slip st to first BPdc.

Rnd 5: Ch 1, (sc, ch 2) twice in same st and in each st around; join with slip st to first sc, finish off. 🐦

GENERAL INSTRUCTIONS

ABBREVIATIONS

BP	Back Post
BPdc	Back Post double crochet(s)
BPdtr	Back Post double treble crochet(s)
BPtr	Back Post treble crochet(s)
ch(s)	chain(s)
cm	centimeters
dc	double crochet(s)
dtr	double treble crochet(s)
exsc	extended single crochet(s)
FP	Front Post
FPdc	Front Post double crochet(s)
FPdtr	Front Post double treble crochet(s)
FPtr	Front Post treble crochet(s)
hdc	half double crochet(s)
mm	millimeters
Rnd(s)	Round(s)
sc	single crochet(s)
sp(s)	space(s)
st(s)	stitch(es)
tr	treble crochet(s)
YO	yarn over

★ — work instructions following ★ as **many more** times as indicated in addition to the first time.

† to † — work all instructions from first † to second † **as many** times as specified.

( ) or [ ] — work enclosed instructions **as many** times as specified by the number immediately following **or** work all enclosed instructions in the stitch or space indicated **or** contains explanatory remarks.

colon (:) — the number(s) given after a colon at the end of a row or round denote(s) the number of stitches or spaces you should have on that row or round.

work even — work without increasing or decreasing in the established pattern.

CROCHET HOOKS													
U.S.	B-1	C-2	D-3	E-4	F-5	G-6	H-8	I-9	J-10	K-10½	N	P	Q
Metric - mm	2.25	2.75	3.25	3.5	3.75	4	5	5.5	6	6.5	9	10	15

■□□□ BEGINNER	Projects for first-time crocheters using basic stitches. Minimal shaping.
■■□□ EASY	Projects using yarn with basic stitches, repetitive stitch patterns, simple color changes, and simple shaping and finishing.
■■■□ INTERMEDIATE	Projects using a variety of techniques, such as basic lace patterns or color patterns, mid-level shaping and finishing.
■■■■ EXPERIENCED	Projects with intricate stitch patterns, techniques and dimension, such as non-repeating patterns, multi-color techniques, fine threads, small hooks, detailed shaping and refined finishing.

GAUGE

Exact gauge is **essential** for proper fit. Before beginning your project, make the sample swatch given in the individual instructions in the yarn and hook specified. After completing the swatch, measure it, counting your stitches and rows carefully. If your swatch is larger or smaller than specified, **make another, changing hook size to get the correct gauge.** Keep trying until you find the size hook that will give you the specified gauge. Once proper gauge is obtained, measure width of the garment approximately every 3" (7.5 cm) to be sure gauge remains consistent.

Yarn Weight Symbol & Names	LACE 0	SUPER FINE 1	FINE 2	LIGHT 3	MEDIUM 4	BULKY 5	SUPER BULKY 6
Type of Yarns in Category	Fingering, 10-count crochet thread	Sock, Fingering Baby	Sport, Baby	DK, Light Worsted	Worsted, Afghan, Aran	Chunky, Craft, Rug	Bulky, Roving
Crochet Gauge* Ranges in Single Crochet to 4" (10 cm)	32-42 double crochets**	21-32 sts	16-20 sts	12-17 sts	11-14 sts	8-11 sts	5-9 sts
Advised Hook Size Range	Steel*** 6,7,8 Regular hook B-1	B-1 to E-4	E-4 to 7	7 to I-9	I-9 to K-10.5	K-10.5 to M-13	M-13 and larger

*GUIDELINES ONLY: The chart above reflects the most commonly used gauges and hook sizes for specific yarn categories.

** Lace weight yarns are usually crocheted on larger-size hooks to create lacy openwork patterns. Accordingly, a gauge range is difficult to determine. Always follow the gauge stated in your pattern.

*** Steel crochet hooks are sized differently from regular hooks–the higher the number the smaller the hook, which is the reverse of regular hook sizing.

CROCHET TERMINOLOGY	
UNITED STATES	INTERNATIONAL
slip stitch (slip st) =	single crochet (sc)
single crochet (sc) =	double crochet (dc)
half double crochet (hdc) =	half treble crochet (htr)
double crochet (dc) =	treble crochet(tr)
treble crochet (tr) =	double treble crochet (dtr)
double treble crochet (dtr) =	triple treble crochet (ttr)
triple treble crochet (tr tr) =	quadruple treble crochet (qtr)
skip =	miss

MARKERS

Markers are used to help distinguish the beginning of each round being worked or for placement of stitch patterns. Place a 2" (5 cm) scrap piece of yarn before the first stitch of each round or around stitch indicated on each row, moving marker after each round or row is complete.

ZEROS

To consolidate the length of an involved pattern, zeros are sometimes used so that all sizes can be combined. For example, increase every sixth row, 5{1-0} time(s) means the first size would increase 5 times, the second size would increase once, and the largest size would do nothing.

JOINING WITH SC

When instructed to join with sc, begin with a slip knot on hook. Insert hook in stitch or space indicated, YO and pull up a loop, YO and draw through both loops on hook.

JOINING WITH BPDC

When instructed to join with BPdc, begin with a slip knot on hook. YO, holding loop on hook, insert hook from **back** to **front** around post of st indicated *(Fig. 4)*, YO and pull up a loop (3 loops on hook), (YO and draw through 2 loops on hook) twice.

BACK RIDGE

Work only in loops indicated by arrows *(Fig. 1)*.

Fig. 1

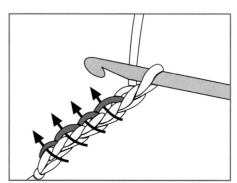

BACK LOOP ONLY

When instructed to work in back loop of a stitch, work in loop(s) indicated by arrow *(Fig. 2)*.

Fig. 2

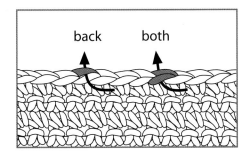

POST STITCH

Work around post of stitch indicated, inserting hook in direction of arrow *(Fig. 4)*.

Fig. 4

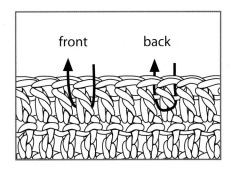

FREE LOOPS OF A CHAIN

When instructed to work in free loops of a chain, work in loops indicated by arrow *(Fig. 3)*.

Fig. 3

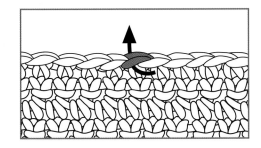

WORKING IN TOP OF A STITCH

When instructed to work into the top of a stitch just made, insert hook in direction of arrow *(Fig. 5)*.

Fig. 5

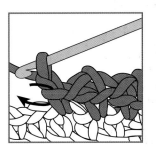

WHIPSTITCH

With **wrong** sides together, sew through both pieces once to secure the beginning of the seam, leaving an ample yarn end to weave in later. Insert the needle from **front** to **back** through both strands on each piece *(Fig. 6a)* **or** through inside loops of each piece *(Fig. 6b)*. Bring the needle around and insert it from **front** to **back** through the next strands on both pieces.

Repeat along the edge, being careful to match stitches and rows.

Fig. 6a

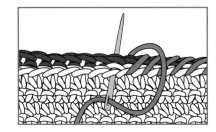

Fig. 6b

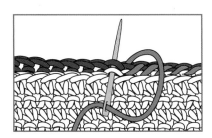